]

THE F

LOMAX

The First Ten Years

The Story of the Lomax Motor Company

By

Tom Lucas

FLYSCREEN PUBLICATIONS

FLYSCREEN PUBLICATIONS
17, Rickyard Close
Stopsley, LUTON, Beds. LU2 9DB
England

First published in 1997
Copyright © 1993, 1994, 1995, 1996, 1997 by Tom Lucas

ISBN 0 9530323 0 2

Printed in Great Britain by White Crescent Press Ltd., Luton

Acknowledgements

Of all the people who have helped or encouraged me in the preparation of this
volume, I would particularly like to thank the following : -

John Brown and Carlton Television - for use of photographs
Reg Bygrave - for his detective work on the fate of the first Lomax kit sold
Citroën UK Ltd - for permission to use photographs
Peter Cook - for the loan of photographs and ephemera
Chris Eker of The Lomax Register - for his reminiscences
Peter Filby - for permission to reproduce material from early editions of 'Kit Car'
Nik François - for the loan of photographs and ephemera
Ian Hyne, editor of 'Kitcars International' - for permission to use photographs and loan
of much valuable material
David Low of Lomax Motor Co. Ltd. - for his reminiscences
Terry Lumley - for disk conversion and scanning
John Nash - for permission to use his cartoons
Mike Nicks and Howard Reynolds of 'Bike' magazine - for use of illustrations
Ewan Scott, editor of 'Kit Car' magazine - for permission to reproduce many photos
Ian Stent, editor of 'Which Kit' magazine - for permission to reproduce photos
David Williams - for specially-commissioned photography
John Wheatley - for providing his excellent cartoons at short notice

And a Special Thank You to

Nigel Whall

For the loan of much unique material, permission to use the same in the book and
allowing me to take up many hours of his time in interviews

If he hadn't have done it, I couldn't have written about it !

To Jay

Contents

Introduction

I FIRST saw it in March 1983. A picture of 'Genesis' - the Lomax prototype. Four headlights and a tiny radiator grille, surmounting what looked like a small aircraft engine, stared out at me from the pages of 'Kit Car' magazine. I sat there staring back in disbelief and wonderment. Love at first sight ! I had to wait four years to acquire one, but it was worth it. All the noise and drama of a large motorcycle but no stuffy crash helmet to wear. The sun on your face and the wind in your hair. Old gents waving their walking sticks as you pass, convinced that you're driving a Morgan trike. You can't beat it. Even after *The First Ten Years* - I'm still in love !

Tom Lucas
January 1997

CYCLE CAR

Gulp! New kit cars are appearing thick and fast — faster, we suspect, than is good for the business. One of the latest to make a bow is the Lomax 224 which echos the cycle car theme of the '20s and early '30s. Based on the Citroen 2CV through Ami 8 range of utility saloons and estates, this equally functional vehicle can be assembled to the standard exhibited in the photograph for £925.75 inc VAT plus the donor car. The complete component package requires a lead time of eight weeks from order. A further £332.50 will purchase a full width screen and a set of weather equipment.

The bodywork is hand moulded using a conventional double skin foam sandwich construction which is extremely rigid. A twin rail steel chassis is employed. With the basic 602cc air cooled flat twin, its output of 40bhp gives a power/weight ratio of approximately 100bhp/tonne. Inspiration for the shape and layout has come from the Morgan trikes with a hint of Type 35 Bugatti in the tail profile.

Other derivatives are under development. The Lomax 223 is a three wheeler with a decided accent on light weight. With an extruded alloy chassis it will weigh only 300 Kg. A third car, the 424, similar to the 224, has its accent on speed and will employ the 1200cc flat four from the GS Citroen range.

Further information on this extraordinary range of kit car can be obtained from **Resinject Developments, Lime Tree House, Long Lane, Willoughton, Gainsborough, DN21 5SQ. Tel: 0427 73 550.**

***Above:* The picture that started it all !**
Photograph reproduced by kind permission of Peter Filby and 'Kit Car' Magazine

CHAPTER ONE
In The Beginning....

THE HISTORY of the mainstream motor industry is populated by individuals who built their empires from small beginnings. Without Henry Ford, there would be no Ford Motor Co. Without H.F.S. Morgan, no Morgan Motor Co., and without Nigel Whall the Lomax would never have seen the light of day.

1.1 **A 1963 photo featuring a youthful Nigel Whall at the wheel of his Morgan 4/4**
Photo: Courtesy of Nigel Whall

Nigel Whall was born in Wolverhampton on 25th April 1946. His formative years were spent in the area, and he stayed there until he left school, having taken several 'O' levels. In 1963, Nigel moved to Lincolnshire with his parents and started his first job as a trainee metallurgist. The eight years between 1963 and 1971 were the only time Nigel spent in someone elses's employ, because for the remainder of his career, Nigel has been self-employed. In the mid-1960's, the Morgan three wheeler had not yet acquired the exclusive image which it enjoys today, and for many, it represented cheap and basic transport. Perhaps Nigel Whall's ownership of a 1937 Morgan F2 trike (purchased for £5 !) during this period provided some of the inspiration when he subsequently designed his own car. The superiority of a good three wheeler over a conventional car was hammered home when he raced a fellow college student to the pub one day - and won ! Nigel's Morgan thoroughly trounced his mate's Mini-van, out-running and finally out-cornering it in a spectacular fashion at the bottom of a steep hill. Before the Morgan trike, Nigel had owned a brace of what would be valuable thoroughbreds today, but were just old sports cars then - a Coventry-Climax engined Morgan 4/4 and an MG TD.

1.2 Nigel Whall's 1935 Morgan F2 (bought in 1966 for £5 !) *right,* Nigel's MG TD
Photo: Courtesy of Nigel Whall

A total change of direction in the early '70s saw Nigel becoming involved with a company making resin injection-moulding equipment. This company was a sub-contractor to the BSA-Norton-Triumph motorcycle empire, and produced large batches of battery boxes and seat pans in the last days of the British motorbike industry. One of the things this company made were the GRP mouldings for the famous limited-edition of 1,000 Triumph X-75 Hurricanes. Designed by an American, Craig Vetter, this was a 750cc Triumph Trident triple with flowing bodywork incorporating the tank and sidepanels. Years ahead of their time, these styling classics haven't dated and still look state-of-the-art today – when you can find one – for they are very rare. Although GRP petrol tanks were considered legal for road use in Britain at that time, and Nigel's firm made these for other (home-market) models, USA regulations banned them. Because it was mainly intended for export, the Hurricane tank was of steel, sandwiched within two glassfibre mouldings. The sad decline of the British bike industry has been well documented, and with the final collapse of BSA-Triumph came the end of the lucrative contracts for GRP.

Time to move on, and this time Nigel set up his own company, Injectoplas, to develop vacuum-injection techniques for larger assemblies. This business lasted until 1980, when it was sold on and a new company was formed, called Resinject Developments Ltd. Unlike Injectoplas, Resinject was begun as a consultancy business, basically a trade name for Nigel's skills. Resinject was (and is) primarily involved in the 'closed mould' method of producing glassfibre components. This is much the same system that Lotus use to produce their car bodies and claim to have invented, although this is open to argument. This subsequently proved to be the case when Lotus set their patent agents onto Resinject and later had to withdraw their contention when

1.3 **The Craig Vetter-designed Triumph X-75 Hurricane**
Illustration by Howard Reynolds, reproduced by kind permission of 'Bike' magazine

it was shown that RDL had prior knowledge of the process. Resinject's forte was to obtain contracts from companies that needed to use this technology but lacked either the resources to develop their own, or the large amounts of money that others were charging for their services. Business went well, and although the contracts were few and far between, they paid handsomely. By mid-1981, Nigel was able to live comfortably and have time to devote to other pursuits.

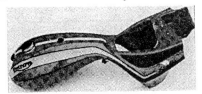

1.4 **The Hurricane tank/seatpan unit that Nigel Whall manufactured**
Photo: reproduced by kind permission of 'Bike' magazine

With time on his hands, and not used to being idle, he started thinking up ideas for a development project for Resinject. A lightweight, complicated monocoque structure was decided upon, with the idea that it could become a showpiece to demonstrate the benefits of the 'vaccuum-injection closed mould' system to potential customers. Because of Nigel's love of lightweight sports cars, the concept of a small sports car that could both serve as a publicity vehicle for Resinject, and at the same time be sold to impecunious young enthusiasts, began to take shape. At this stage, the idea was something rather along the lines of the Frogeye Sprite, powered by a low-capacity air-cooled engine - possibly a motorcycle power unit of 250-300cc. A top speed of around 80mph was envisaged, which together with good handling, would ensure reasonable insurance costs for the intended market.

One of Resinject's contracts was with Terrapin International in Milton Keynes. Terrapin had a subsidiary that made shower units for use in hotel rooms with an en-suite facility, and it was Resinject's brief to produce the tooling for the shower trays. The man in charge of the shower unit project was to take Nigel for a business lunch, but unfortunately his car was being repaired and his temporary transport turned out to be a rather down-at-heel Citroen 2CV. Because he had to leave immediately after lunch, Nigel followed in his own car. All was not well with the 2CV, and it soon began firing on only one cylinder. The chap stopped and lifted the bonnet, and more out of curiosity than anything else, Nigel joined him as he began his investigations into the mysteries of French electrics. It was then that he noticed the air-cooling fins around the spark-plug hole as the chap was working. Until that moment, Nigel hadn't really noticed the 2CV, let alone realised that it possessed an air-cooled motor. After the meeting, he went straight home and got a book from the local library about the 2CV and its derivatives. The book contained a cross-section of the engine and transmission and Nigel realised that at last he had found the power unit he had been looking for. That evening, Nigel scanned the local paper and saw an Ami 8 for sale, about twenty miles from his Gainsborough home. It had been involved in an accident and had been rolled, as well as shunted front and rear, but was largely complete and advertised at only £30. Nigel's wife drove him to the vendor, money changed hands, and he became the owner of a very battered Citroën. It was about 9.00pm and there weren't many people about, so Nigel elected to drive his new acquisition home. On the way, he decided to see how his purchase performed and was most surprised to extract 75mph from it ! The following day, Nigel Whall began to strip the Ami down. Although the chassis proved to be bent, it was quite noticeable that it was well preserved, and the modular construction of the car soon became apparent. The fact that major sub-assemblies, like the front suspension, could be removed by simply undoing a few bolts meant that they could be easily transferred to another vehicle - of any shape. All the elements of the sports car were there. The engine was air-cooled and of low capacity, the suspension could be relocated in its entirety, even the pedal box was a neat self-contained unit which could easily be placed on a different bulkhead.

One by one, the original ideas of monocoque, motorcycle engine, and a self-built suspension system (which was also part of the original plan) went by the board. During the period when Nigel was working out the first concept, he produced a number of styling sketches. When these were combined with the dimensions imposed by the Citroën mechanical base, such as track, wheelbase and engine height, the basic shape of the car quickly began to emerge. At that time, Nigel owned a Triumph TR6, and the cockpit measurements for the new car were based around this, purely because it fitted the bill and was readily available. Although he had no formal training in draughtsmanship, Nigel produced a design drawing which was scaled up to full size, and he then set to in his garage at home to produce the styling buck. Although the body design was finalised and created quite quickly, the styling of the front end caused more than a few headaches. Some three months were spent making a bonnet buck which resembled the Morris Eight Series 'E'. When it emerged into the light of day, it looked far too bulky, and so Nigel destroyed it and started again.

1.5 An artist's impression of the abortive Lomax 224

Drawing: Nik François

The second time around, the tactic of first covering the engine with expanded polyurethane foam, and then carving it back to produce a closely-tailored front, paid off. As any Lomax owner today will testify, the engine *is* a very tight fit under the bonnet. The resultant bonnet closely resembled that of the present Lomax, with the important difference that the front cowling and bonnet were separate mouldings - these were later to become a single entity. A styling idea tried - and rejected - was a thin vertical bar

running down the centre of the dummy radiator grille. With the styling buck complete, a mould, and then the first body was produced, in black. The car hadn't been named yet, and one evening Nigel was laying in bed thinking idly, "If I could choose another surname, what would I like to be called ?". Nigel decided on 'Lomax', purely because he liked the sound of it, and Lomax subsequently became the name of the car. Later in the car's existence it was ventured that the name stood for LOw cost – MAXimum speed, but it never caught on.

1.6 This specially-sectioned Lomax shows the close proximity of the engine to the bonnet   *Photo: reproduced by kind permission of 'Kitcars International' magazine*

1.7 Two views of the Lomax 224 body buck nearing completion

Photos: Courtesy of Nigel Whall

1.8 A detail shot of the Genesis rear mudguard bracket *(above)* and dashboard *(below)*
Photos: *Courtesy of Nigel Whall*

CHAPTER TWO
Genesis

THE VERY first Lomax, subsequently nicknamed 'Genesis', was quite different to the Lomax that is in production today. The prototype was some 17½ inches shorter than the present car, 11½ inches being added to the cockpit area and approximately 2½ inches to both scuttle and boat-tail in subsequent mouldings. At least some of this extra length was due to the fact that 'Genesis' sat on a fabricated ladder chassis rather than a Citroën one, and therefore enjoyed a considerably shorter wheelbase than its modern counterpart. 'Genesis' differed in other ways too. The suspension was supported not by the Citroën spring canisters, but by rubber cones sourced from a Mini. Naturally, the car had a wheel in each corner – the three wheeler version hadn't been thought of at this stage. Because of this, it had the 'letterbox' rear end, which was carried over to the first forty or so kits that were sold. The 'letterbox' consisted of an aperture moulded two-thirds of the way down the boat-tail, into which the spare wheel was inserted, as seen on the Healey Silverstone. Not only was this a convenient way of storing the spare, but of course it acted as a rear bumper too. The wheel was positioned so that it bore against the rear axle, and in the event of a rear-end collision, the tyre and wheel would form a superb deformable structure. The petrol tank was mounted above, set into the boot floor. Like any prototype, this car was built far more strongly than was strictly necessary. For instance, the rear section of the boat-tail was double-skinned and incorporated six inches of polyurethane foam. This double-skinning extended as far as the sides of the cockpit and resulted in a very robust structure.

2.1 'Genesis' undergoing trials at Hillstow Airfield in spring 1982
Photo: Courtesy of Nigel Whall

'Genesis' was built up fairly quickly, but wasn't registered for the road for a while. The problem of being able to drive the car legally, in order to be able to road test it, was solved by taking it to the deserted go-kart track at nearby Hillstow Airfield during the week. The car was quite a regular visitor to Hillstow during the spring of 1982, and usually arrived there on the back of a farm trailer loaned by a friend. Details such as mudguards were added, and so were the Bugatti-style wheel trims which still adorn the present-day Lomax.

2.2 Two views of the unfinished 'Genesis' at Nigel Whall's Lincolnshire home. The mudguards, wheel trims and lighting are not yet finalised

Photos: Courtesy of Nigel Whall

2.3 A detail shot of the 'Genesis' nosecone. Note the nearside-mounted alternator

Photo: Courtesy of Nigel Whall

The Lomax body is not a particularly easy shape to mould in fibreglass, but this shape was specifically chosen to give the impression that it was constructed from metal. Although the casual onlooker can see the lines of many famous cars echoed in the Lomax, e.g. Morgan or Healey Silverstone, from some angles the car has overtones of Bugatti. This was not lost on Nigel, and Bugatti-style wheel trims were moulded from the most unlikely of sources – the cast base of an old-fashioned swivelling office chair with the wheel from a child's toy set into the centre ! Nigel Whall's main aim was to build the car as a showpiece for Resinject Developments, and for his own satisfaction, with only a vague idea of selling replicas, so he wasn't totally prepared for what happened next.

2.4 **A newly-completed 'Genesis'**

Photo: Courtesy of Nigel Whall

CITROEN TRANSFORMED

3.1 *Above:* The first published article on the Lomax 224 appeared in the now–defunct *'Sports Car Mechanics'* magazine.

CHAPTER THREE
Into Production

BY SUMMER 1982, Genesis was reaching the road-ready stage. A twin exhaust system was made by filling the pipes with sand, then heating and bending them to shape. The headlamp system consisted of four spotlamps from a local car accessory shop. These were wired so that two provided main beam, and the other pair, suitably angled downwards, gave dip. Nigel claims that it isn't easy to get *anything* in Lincolnshire, and this included stand-alone headlamps ! Electrical power was courtesy of an alternator mounted low down on the nearside. At last the car was registered, like almost every Lomax since, with the donor's original number - 'MBP 821 J'.

Someone spotted Genesis and tipped off a (now-defunct) magazine called 'Sportscar Mechanics', who duly sent out a reporter to see the car. He had a ride in it, liked it, and wrote a complimentary article, entitled 'Citroën Transformed'. Within a very short time, over five hundred enquiries arrived in the post ! Obviously, Genesis had struck a chord with the buying public. Selling true replicas of Genesis wasn't really on, because of the added complication of producing the chassis in quantity, so a compromise was reached, and the Genesis body was stretched to fit the stock Citroën chassis by inserting an extra 11½ inches into the cockpit. Even then, as Nigel freely admits, the car hadn't been developed as a kit car at that stage, and the first customers received the glassfibre parts only - plus an Ami handbrake bracket. The fact that this left the customer to make all his own metalwork did not deter people overmuch. In fact, it seemed that everyone had twenty-five Citroën rolling chassis under wraps, just waiting for the Lomax to be introduced ! A local GRP moulder was sub-contracted to make the bodies, and Nigel was in the kit car business.

3.2 A pair of early Lomax 224 kits awaiting despatch. Note the undertrays propped behind the body tubs. *Photo: Courtesy of Nigel Whall*

3.3 *Overleaf:* An early Lomax brochure

Courtesy of Lomax Motor Co. Ltd.

LOMAX MOTOR COMPANY

~~LIMETREE HOUSE,~~
~~HUNTERS ROAD,~~
~~HOCKLEY,~~
~~BIRMINGHAM,~~
~~B19 1EB~~
~~Tel. 021 233 3308~~

* ★ **RIGID GRP BODY IN PRIMER GREY PIGMENT**
* ★ **EXPOSED AIR COOLED ENGINE**
* ★ **ALL ROUND INDEPENDENT SUSPENSION**
* ★ **FRONT WHEELED DRIVE**
* ★ **SUPERB ROAD HOLDING**
* ★ **GOOD PERFORMANCE AND ECONOMY**
* ★ **EASILY ASSEMBLED**

The very first Lomax body, in red, was sold in late '82 to Mr. Peter Jackson, proprietor of Brampton Garage, a Citroën dealership in Huntingdon. Even at this stage, he had plans to fit the Ami Super engine. Nigel was unaware of the Ami Super's existence until he heard of Mr. Jackson's plans, and the idea was noted. Much later, this was revived to become the Lomax 424. Ironically, this first customer's car was probably never completed. The front was altered to take the Citroën flat four, but work progressed fitfully, and when Brampton Garage closed down, the car was acquired by Pleiades of Sawtry, along with most of the spare parts stock. Pleiades kept the car for a while, by now on Dyane running gear, then sold the car on in 1987, still half-built. The customer apparently passed the car on to his brother-in-law, who eventually sold it - still incomplete ! Tantalisingly, from there on the trail goes cold.

Initially available in just three colours - black, red or blue - approximately forty Lomax 224s of this type were sold between late 1982 and spring 1983. A particular feature of these cars was a fibreglass undertray which went from behind the front numberplate, and down the sides of the chassis, finishing behind the driveshafts. The bulkhead was different to that of the current Lomax, in that the passenger's footwell was slightly shorter, with the battery being mounted on a 'shelf' above, rather than the top of the footwell.

3.4 The 'Mock 223' undergoing construction. The bodyshell in the background has the truncated passenger footwell that is a trademark of the first Lomax 224s.

Photo: Courtesy of Nigel Whall

Early in 1983, it became apparent that Nigel would have to call in some outside help to run the Lomax side of his business. He was becoming busier with his consultancy work, and was being pressurized by one of his major customers, M & G Trailers, to work for them four days per week instead of two. At the same time, he was attempting to deal with a large number of enquiries for the Lomax while being let down by the sub-contractor in Lincolnshire who was making the bodies. Nigel decided that the best course of action would be to hand the day-to-day running of the Lomax project over to someone else, and perhaps take a share of the profits at the end of each year. This would leave him free to concentrate on his original line of work and, (since M & G were by now offering generous moving expenses) organise a relocation to the Birmingham area. Flicking through a kit car magazine one day, Nigel came across a letter from a Mr. Peter Bird. Peter Bird was a designer with previous automotive experience who had worked on the ill-fated Stevens Cypher, a pretty little sports car based on Reliant Kitten mechanicals. Nigel wrote and made an appointment to see him, and was surprised to find that he was in business in a much smaller way than he had expected. At this time, Peter was working from a Birmingham City Council Enterprise Starter Unit (about the size of a double garage) in the Sparkbrook area. He already had a contract to mould wings for another kit car manufacturer, and seemed very enthusiastic. Peter and Nigel reached an agreement, and Peter's firm, Falcon Automotive, took on the manufacture and marketing of the Lomax, together with a bank account containing the customers' deposits that had been collected so far.

3.5 Side view of the 'Mock 223'. Note the complete absence of rear light pods.
Photograph reproduced by kind permission of Peter Filby and 'Kit Car' magazine.

Lomax's first public appearance was at the Lincoln International Component Car Show (predecessor to Stoneleigh) in April 1983. Genesis was on the stand, accompanied by the first Lomax 223, registered 'NFT 896 P'. However, this was not a true three wheeler, since the wheel configuration was achieved by turning the rear trailing arms inwards, giving two rear wheels inches from each other beneath the boat tail. Like Genesis, this car was also a one-off, for it was soon discovered that, in the eyes of the law, it was not a tricycle. With the Lincoln Show coming up, the 'three wheeler' was built in a matter of weeks on Dyane running gear. The original moulding was modified by deleting the 'letter box' tyre slot in the rear, and moulding in a small box-cum-numberplate bracket instead. This was made necessary by the fact that the body was shorter than that of the present-day Lomax, the rear tyres protruding into the numberplate box to compensate ! A contemporary article in a kit car magazine said of this arrangement: 'When asked about the non-fitment of a spare wheel, Nigel simply pointed to the twin rear wheels, and stated that there is an "active" spare wheel which can continue to work away at the back until it is required. Should a front wheel need replacing, the driver simply takes off one of the rear wheels, and puts it on the front ! Furthermore, if a rear tyre is punctured, it can be left in place until it is convenient to change it. A novel arrangement to say the least !'. It was quite noticeable that most people who visited the stand were showing an interest in the 'three wheeler', rather than Genesis. Possibly this influenced the decision to stretch the Lomax again in order to produce a dual-purpose body that would serve for both the 223 and 224, and later the 424.

3.6 Dorian Dandridge's immaculately-preserved 224 exhibits all the tell-tale features of the early cars – this front view shows the undertray behind the number plate, the absence of an oil cooler slot and no alternator bulge...... *Photo: Author*

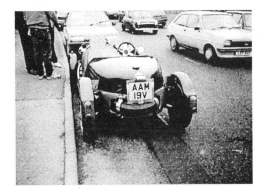

3.7 ....Rear view shows the characteristic 'letterbox' for the spare wheel...........
Photo: Author

3.8 ....And this view shows the extent of the front undertray.
Photo: Author

3.9 (above) The characteristic 'battery shelf' and truncated passenger footwell of the early cars and *(below)* The arrows show the areas in which the extra length was added to the cockpit by extending the 'Genesis' moulding   *Photos: Author*

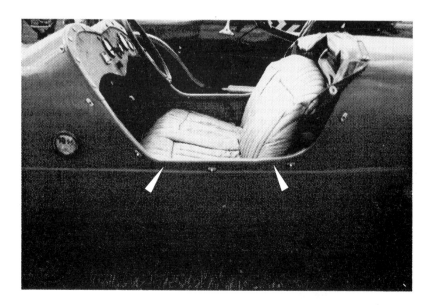

CHAPTER FOUR
The Year of the Falcon

BY JUNE 1983, the Lomax moulds were in Peter Bird's possession and the Lomax Motor Co. was under way. A trial body was moulded by Peter at his Sparkbrook workshop, but this proved unsatisfactory and had to be scrapped. By September, the Lomax Motor Co. had moved to larger premises at 222, Livery Street, Birmingham and staff had been hired. By this time, about twenty bodies had been moulded by the Lincolnshire sub-contractor and sold by Nigel, and approximately fourteen of the same type were in the pipeline at Lomax to satisfy outstanding orders. Peter and his staff were experiencing problems with the moulds, which by now were beginning to wear, and had difficulty producing reasonable bodies from them. Even as early as this, Lomax had their eye to the export market, one body going to Cyprus and others to Holland. The first Lomax overseas agent was classic car dealer Aris Motor Co. of Valkenburg ZH., appointed in October 1983. There were problems with one of the bodies supplied to them, and following a trip to Holland to exchange it, Nigel hired premises near to the present Lomax works, and employed two experienced moulders to produce the bodies there. These two were later to go on to work for Westfield Sports Cars.

4.1 This promotional champagne bottle label was produced for the Dutch Lomax agent
Courtesy of Nigel Whall

This seemed to solve the quality problem, and freed from the constraints of fibreglass moulding, Peter Bird was able to concentrate further upon readying the design for quantity production. One of the first changes was to the front end of the car, making the bonnet as one piece instead of two, adding the slot for the oil cooler and incorporating a bulge on the offside for the repositioned alternator. At the same time, the undertray beneath the bonnet was dispensed with. The 'Mock 223' prototype was a 'halfway house' between the old Lomax and the new, carrying the old style bonnet, but with an oil cooler slot cut out below the dummy radiator grille to modernize its appearance. As Peter worked on the front end of the car, Nigel was changing the design of the body tub to allow it to be used as a dual purpose three wheeler/four wheeler.

The body was stretched once again, this time 2½" being added at the scuttle and a further 2½" at the boat tail. The shape of the rear of the boat tail was dramatically altered below the waistline. The letterbox slot was deleted, and pods for the rear lights added. This had the effect of making the pronounced waistline ledge into a shallow coach line. At the scuttle, the nearside 'battery shelf' was turned into a full passenger footwell. If you examine the front bulkhead of any modern Lomax, the joint line can still be seen. The body produced by these modifications became that of the kit you can buy today.

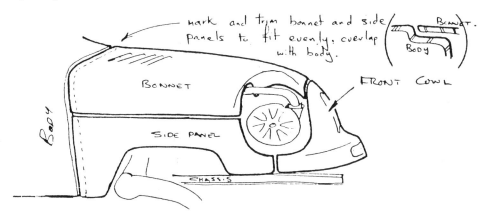

4.2 **This extract from the 1983 Lomax build manual clearly shows the contemporary bonnet, nosecone and side panels.** *Illustration: Courtesy of Lomax Motor Co. Ltd.*

Up until this time, the Lomax had been sold as fibreglass parts only, so Peter Bird set to and designed a range of metalwork for the car. This included the headlamp and mudguard brackets, but not the scuttle frame, which was a later development. Peter also developed a set of weather equipment, which included a fixed windscreen. This was manufactured from an 'E' section aluminium extrusion with a web on the back, and was the same as that supplied with a contemporary beach-buggy kit, the Kingfisher Kustom.

4.3 **An original Kingfisher Kustom beach-buggy.** **The same windscreen, fitted with an aluminium valance panel, was sold for use with the Lomax.** *Photo: Author*

The first true Lomax three wheeler was, in fact, built by a customer and it was he who came up with the idea of turning one of the rear suspension arms inwards and welding in an extension behind the hub to bring the wheel to the centre. This arrangement was adopted by Lomax, and in early 1984, Peter Bird constructed the first Lomax 223 demonstrator, in green. At this time Ami 8 donors were still quite plentiful, and because the Ami comes equipped with large spring cannisters and heavy-duty springs, the single-sided rear suspension worked well. It was only much later, when the more lightly-sprung Dyane and 2CV became the usual donor, that this arrangement had to have additional stiffening. A little-known fact is that the Lomax Motor Co. were also listed in at least one current kit car magazine as being the manufacturers of the Stevens Cypher. It is unclear whether any 'Lomax' Cyphers were ever produced.

4.4 Two views of the 'counterfeit' Lomax at Mr. Richard Pratt's home. **Note the 'blank' dashboard.** *Photos: Courtesy of Nigel Whall*

It was around this time that relations between Nigel and Peter became somewhat strained, and Nigel began to think about terminating their business partnership. During this period, Nigel met Brian Mumford, creator of the Vauxhall-engined Mumford Musketeer three wheeler, at a kit car show. The Lomax stand was attracting a lot of attention from the public, whilst on the Mumford stand things were pretty stagnant. Over the course of the weekend, Nigel and Brian got talking, and Brian expressed an interest in taking on production of the Lomax range. With Brian Mumford waiting in the wings to take over, Nigel wrote a letter to Peter Bird terminating their partnership, and a new Lomax Motor Co. *Ltd*. was formed with Nigel and Brian as directors. But things didn't quite work out as easily as that.

At this time, Peter Bird was still, naturally, trading as the Lomax Motor Co. and had some fourteen firm orders for cars on the books. To expedite matters, Nigel suggested either handing the orders over to Mumford or returning the customers' deposits. While Peter prevaricated, metalwork production transferred to Brian Mumford's premises at Nailsworth, Glos., and fibreglass production was put in the hands of a sub-contractor called Hunting Glassfibre at Tetbury. Then one day Nigel received a 'phone call from a chap called Richard Pratt, who was having problems assembling his car. Nigel could not recall a customer of that name, and asked him when and where he had bought his kit. He replied that it had been supplied by Peter Bird and when he mentioned the date of purchase, Nigel realised that it was some time after he had officially ended the agreement. So where had Peter got the kit from ? Nigel was soon to find out, when he made an appointment to see Mr. Pratt. There on Mr. Pratt's drive was a green Lomax bodyshell, only it hadn't been manufactured by Lomax. The main difference was that the instrument pod had been omitted from the dashboard, which was instead a flat panel. It differed in other, more subtle, ways but that was the main identifying feature. It was pretty obvious that Peter had taken a mould from one of the last genuine Lomax bodyshells that he had supplied, and Nigel was not pleased.

Nigel asked Mr. Pratt for an affidavit, and immediately sought legal advice. A permanent injunction was granted against Peter Bird restraining him from making or selling any further counterfeit Lomax bodies or using the word 'Lomax', and the court made Peter surrender the front portion of the mould to Nigel. It was never discovered how many counterfeit Lomax bodies had been made, although it is thought that the total may have crept into double figures. By Summer 1984, Peter Bird's connection with Lomax was finally severed, and Peter went on to design and produce the Lotus Seven-inspired, Citroën-powered Falcon. A three wheeler version of this car was subsequently produced with a fibreglass boat tail – bearing more than a passing resemblance to that of the Lomax !

4.4 Peter Bird went on to design and produce the Lotus Seven-inspired, Citroën-powered Falcon in both four and three-wheeled forms

Illustrations Courtesy of Peter Bird

Model 424

Model 424

The LOMAX 424 is based on the Ami Super which uses the GS engine and gearbox. The kit consists of Body Tub, one piece bonnet, two front cycle wings, two rear cycle wings and four wheel trims. As per the 224 and 223 models, all GRP is available in colour impregnated resin.

The engine, gearbox and exhaust is unaltered thus saving time and expense in building with the rest of the brackets being as per the 224 model.

With the approximate 55 bhp available and a noticeable reduction in weight, the 424 produces sports car performance and handling with modest economy.

5.1 This circa 1985 Mumford brochure featured the Lomax 424 for the first time
Courtesy of Lomax Motor Co.

CHAPTER FIVE
The Mumford Period

BY JUNE 1984, only a year after the inauguration of the first Lomax Motor Co. (with Peter Bird), production was in the hands of Brian Mumford at Gigg Mill, Nailsworth, and the second incarnation of Lomax, this time as a limited company, had begun. Along with all the tooling etc., came 'Genesis', still doing sterling service as a demonstrator, and a prepared rolling chassis on which the prototype 424 was to be built. It was decided that this model was to share the body tub with the 223 and 224, although at this stage the bonnet design was yet to be finalised. Brian constructed the first 424 *sans* bonnet, and as the shape of the engine compartment developed, Nigel was able to take measurements and produce the new front end. The buck was made by taking a standard 223/224 item and cutting and extending it until it fitted. From this a mould was taken. By September 1985, the 424 was officially part of the Lomax range. Finally, the Lomax body tub was modified to give two new options - opening doors and a removeable panel on the boat-tail allowing a dickey seat to be fitted. However, the 424 demonstator was never completed at Nailsworth because Brian was side-tracked onto building a new three wheeler demonstrator instead.

It was at Gigg Mill that 'Q 508 FAD' first saw the light of day. 'Q-FAD' as most people call her, was built up using a grey primer bodyshell that was intended for one of the last of Peter Bird's customers. It was never established for whom the shell was intended, and so it became surplus to requirements. Some readers may remember 'Q-FAD' as a metallic silver car, but it only acquired this colour much later in its career. It was originally sprayed dark blue. 'Q-FAD' didn't displace 'Genesis' immediately, but as public interest was largely centred on the 223, 'Genesis' was used less and less and started to gather dust at the back of the workshop. A customer asked to buy the car, and as it had served its purpose as far as Nigel was concerned, it was sold off. The chap did half-jokingly suggest that he would return in a few years' time and make a killing by selling the prototype back to the company, but Nigel wasn't interested. After all, if he wanted another 'Genesis', he could easily manufacture one ! 'Genesis' departed to start a new life and after a while was swapped for an Ami estate and some cash. The car's third owner then renamed her 'Tatty Apple'. 'Tatty' because by that time she was, and 'Apple' because she was the apple of his eye ! The car was later crashed and repaired, and after changing hands yet again, survives to this day in the Cheltenham area.

The Lomax bracketry was further refined by Brian, and a brazed-up exhaust system, using Citroën parts, was developed. At the same time, further work went into the weather gear. A distinguishing feature of these Mumford-produced cars was the headlight frame, which was of much thicker material than the present one and was intended to mount direct to the bumper holes on the front rail of the Citroën chassis. This frame was without the bracing to the top of the chassis found on current-production frames. Brian was an excellent engineer, but not really a salesman, and in the first year only two dozen or so kits were produced and sold.

In January 1986, Lomax received some welcome publicity from the now-defunct 'Kitcars and Specials' magazine. A Glasgow-based enthusiast and Citroën specialist, Graham Harper, had been campaigning a tuned letterbox Lomax 224 in Scottish sprints and hillclimbs - and beating sports cars of double the engine capacity. Furthermore, it was being used on the road for delivering Citroën parts, to the tune of 200 miles each week ! The photos accompanying the article show a mid-blue car fitted with

MOTOR COMPANY

LOMAX 224 BODY KIT

ENGINE
: 602cc. Flat twin cylinder air cooled.
Max. B.H.P. 37 B.H.P. @ 5750 R.P.M.
Separate air cooler.

TRANSMISSION
: Four forward gears, synchro 2nd, 3rd and 4th.

BRAKES
: Front inboard disc brakes.
Rear drum brakes.

SUSPENSION
: Independent all round, front leading arm.
Rear trailing arm, coil springs and telescopic shock absorbers all round.

BODY
: G.R.P. with double skin reinforcement.
Cycle type wings and louvred bonnet.

CHASSIS
: "A" series chassis from 2CV, DYANE or AMI.

Registered Office   Directors: B. MUMFORD   J. F. MUMFORD   Registered in England No. 88.7144

GIGG MILL - NAILSWORTH - GLOS. - GL6 OJW   -   -   Tel. 045 383 3170

5.2 A contemporary Lomax brochure   *Courtesy of Lomax Motor Co.*

LOMAX MOTOR COMPANY

SEPTEMBER 1985

No.	Item	Price	223	224	424
001	Oil Cooler mtg.brkt.	2.85	√	√	
002	Alternator mtg.brkt.	2.20	√	√	
003	Fan Belt	4.00	√	√	
004	Modified Oil Filler (Exchange)	24.20	√	√	
005	Oil Cooler Pipe (High press.hose)	1.75 each	√	√	
006	Headlight mtg. frame	19.87	√	√	
007	Headlamp mtg. brkt. L.H.	6.37			√
008	Headlamp mtg. brkt R.H.	6.37			√
009	Front mudguard brkt. L.H.	18.25	√	√	√
010	Front mudguard brkt. R.H.	18.25	√	√	√
011	Hand brake pivot brkt. (disc brake)	5.27	√	√	√
012	Exhaust Manifold pipe L.H.	P.O.A.	√	√	
013	Exhaust manifold pipe R.H.	P.O.A.	√	√	
014	Internal Scuttle Frame	25.00	√	√	√
015	Lengthening Steering Column (Exch.)	5.00	√	√	√
016	Lengthening Suspension eye bolt (rear)	4.00	√	√	√
017	Seat belt anchorage frame	40.00	√	√	√
018	Rear Mudguard brkt. L.H.	5.10		√	
019	Rear Mudguard brkt R.H.	5.10		√	
020	Rear Mudguard brkt. L.H.	4.95			√
021	Rear Mudguard brkt R.H.	4.95			√
022	Rear Bumper black	22.50		√	√
023	Rear Bumper stainless steel	35.00		√	√
024	Louvred Valence	7.50		√	√
025	Gear Linkage assy. (floor change)	14.60	√	√	
026	Gear Linkage Assy. (floor change)	6.00			√
027	Gear Lever Pedestal	9.75			√
028	Bonnet Belt - leather	P.O.A.	√	√	
029	Spare wheel belt	P.O.A.	√	√	√
030	Steering Wheel boss conversion	P.O.A.	√	√	√
031	Seat FrameKit untrimmed	30.00 pair	√	√	√
032	Seats trimmed	100.00 each	√	√	√
033	Spare wheel carrier	20.50	√	√	√
034	Wheel trim	10.85 each	√	√	√
035	Tonneau Cover	49.50	√	√	√
036	Headlights	50.00 pair	√	√	√
037	Aero Screen	35.00 each	√	√	√
038	Windscreen frame incl.rubber seal (full width)	75.00	√	√	√
039	Hood & sidescreens	P.O.A.	√	√	√
040	Carpet	50.00	√	√	√
041	Weldmesh grill	3.00	√	√	
042	Stainless steel exhaust cover				
043	Rear mudguard		√		

I enclose cash/cheque for £ _____
deposit and will pay balance by cash or
Bankers Draft upon collection.
N.B. Price and specification subject to
change without notice.

Body shell light grey   495.00
Bonnet and nose cowl
Engine side panels
Cycle wings
Wheel trims

Colour impreg (State colour) _____ 60.00

TOTAL	£	
VAT		
TOTAL incl. VAT	£	
Deposit paid 20% minimum		
Balance due	£	

Name _____

Address _____

_____

_____

Signed _____ Date _____

GIGG MILL, NAILSWORTH, GLOS. GL6 0JW.   Telephone: 045 383 3170

5.3 **This September 1985 price list shows the full range of brackets and accessories available at the time.**   *Courtesy of Lomax Motor Co.*

Citroën GS wheeltrims instead of the usual Lomax items. Other modifications included resiting the standard 2CV petrol tank beneath the boot floor and blocking off the 'letter-box' with a home-made GRP panel. But most interesting of all were the engine modifications that had been made. Possibly this was the first time someone had attempted to tune a Lomax. The standard carburettor had been discarded, a pair of siamesed items from a Yamaha XS500 motorcycle being fitted instead. Eight pounds had been machined from the flywheel, and a special cam (formula Ford profile) had found its way into the engine. The exhaust system was a home-brewed twin system with a front balance pipe, and the car was fast - very fast.

5.4 The Mumford Musketeer - Brian Mumford's *other* product.   *Photo: Author*

5.5 A rare shot of 'Genesis' and 'Q-FAD' together. By this time, 'Genesis' was in **private ownership.**   *Photo: Peter Cook*

5.6 **This close-up shows the 'Genesis' lamp bracket.** **The sidelights are either side of the number plate, indicators below the headlamps.** *Photo: Peter Cook*

Meanwhile, the first attempt at organising a Lomax register or owners club was made by Mr. Ian Reid of Saltford, near Bristol. In April 1986, he sent a circular letter to several Lomax customers in the Bristol/Bath area, whose addresses had been provided by Brian Mumford. Following a letter in '2CVGB News', the magazine of the Deux Chevaux Club of Great Britain, owners from further afield contacted him. It seems, however, that his efforts came to nought, because all that remains of this early collective is a handful of letters on file at the present Lomax Register.

5.7 **'Q-FAD' on show wearing dark blue livery...................**

Photo: Peter Cook

5.8 ....And the official catalogue picture which was used until 1988 !

Photo: Courtesy of Lomax Motor Co.

Towards the end of 1986, Nigel received a 'phone call from Brian Mumford. Disheartened by slow sales and the general aggravation of running Lomax, Mumford wanted out. It was an amicable parting, and Nigel bought back Brian Mumford's part of the business. Although no longer a director of Lomax, Brian Mumford was to continue to manufacture all the Lomax metalwork for some time to come. As mentioned previously, fibreglass manufacture was in the hands of Hunting Glassfibre at Tetbury, and the Lomax bodies produced during this time were of excellent quality. The Hunting bodies can be readily identified by the paper rope which was moulded into the inside of the top of the boat-tail, just behind the seats. Later bodies substituted a balsa-wood section for this. The bonnet mould used during this period, and for some time at Lye, contained a small defect. This was a brush hair, or similar, which had found its way onto the buck and was subsequently transferred to the mould. Each bonnet from this mould carries a reproduction of the hair in the gel-coat, near the front on the passenger's side. These 'hairs' have sometimes been removed by owners when rubbing down the joint lines on the bodywork.

CHAPTER SIX
All Roads Lead to Lye

JANUARY 1987 saw Nigel Whall back to square one again as far as Lomax was concerned. His increasing workload at M & G Trailers left little time for Lomax activities, and as yet he hadn't made any significant amount of money out of the project. Thoroughly fed up, he cast around for a partner to run Lomax on a day to day basis as before. One of the people he wrote to was a gentleman who manufactured AC Cobra lookalikes. The gent replied to Nigel's letter in a very rude fashion, along the lines that he wouldn't be seen dead involved with a tacky product like the Lomax. A few months later, he disappeared with a large amount of his customers' money - and the Fraud Squad in hot pursuit ! Perhaps Nigel had a lucky escape !

Then Dave Low became involved in the Lomax story. Born on 17th December 1941, Dave spent his early years in London, becoming a keen motorcyclist in his youth. He joined the Royal Navy straight from school, spending five years as a Radio/Electro-Mechanic (Air), working on aircraft aboard aircraft carriers. On leaving the service, Dave went to work for Plessey where he progressed from the shop floor through to production management. Having achieved this, he went on to work for Berry Magicoal and, after several other moves, was finally the production manager at M & G Trailers' fibreglass shop when he met Nigel Whall. Nigel was on the 'phone to a possible Lomax partner, and Dave couldn't help but overhear, so he asked Nigel what this Lomax business was all about. When Nigel explained over the course of several tea-breaks, Dave became very interested. Up until then, the 2CV had merely been a strange little car that he had seen abroad during his naval career, but now he began to see the potential. Dave had some money to spare, so he duly bought into the business and became a 50% partner in the Lomax Motor Co. Ltd.

6.1 **Premises, premises ! The Layland Bros. Garage at Hayes Lane**

Photo: Author

Because Nigel was obviously busy, and Dave was holding down a full-time job at M & G, it was decided to run Lomax as a part-time enterprise, evenings and weekends only. There were to be no manufacturing facilities; instead everything would be made by outside contractors. Brian Mumford was quite happy to continue supplying the metalwork, and the body moulds were brought back to the West Midlands and placed in the hands of a competent local sub-contractor called S & L. Almost opposite M & G Trailers in Hayes Lane, Lye, was a small garage and petrol station run by the two Layland brothers. The garage had a small showroom behind the pumps, capable of housing three or four cars. Ideal premises ! An agreement was reached with the Laylands for the use of the showroom and some space in the garage workshop behind. Alongside the forecourt was a row of lock-up garages, and some of these were pressed into service as storage for Lomax components. The problem of manning the showroom during the week, when Dave and Nigel were working, was neatly solved by making the Layland Brothers the first Lomax agents. Therefore, any weekend sales were 'house', and any weekday sales were 'agents', on which the brothers received commission.

At least one contemporary kit car magazine referred to Lawrence King as a co-director of Lomax in early 1987. Ten years on, all can now be revealed. Mr.L.King was none other than Dave Low under a pseudonym ! The reason for this being that Dave's employers, M & G, would have been rather unhappy had they known about his involvement with Lomax. 'Lawrence' was chosen because Dave was a 'Lawrence of Arabia' fan, and 'King' because it was his wife's maiden name. As an aside, there was a precedent for this. The founder of Littlewoods pools did the self-same thing because *he* didn't want his employer to find out either !

6.2 The 1987 Lomax demonstrator fleet
Photo by Ian Hyne, reproduced by kind permission of Kit Car magazine

With premises sorted out, it was time to freshen up the demonstration fleet and start promoting Lomax properly. 'Q-FAD' the 223, was stripped and rebuilt, and was sent out for a re-paint, changing her colour from dark blue to metallic silver, with red trim. The Red 424 'Q 378 VWP', which Brian Mumford had started building at Nailsworth, was finally completed and featured the three-piece bonnet (although it wasn't long before a one-piece bonnet was developed), flared apron-style front wings, a fibreglass-framed vee windscreen and some natty chromed nine-spoked wheels. The two demonstration cars provided an excellent showpiece for Lomax, showing all the options available at the time - three wheels or four, two cylinders or four cylinders, doors or not, dickey seat, cycle or flared wings and so on.

Up until that time, press coverage had been rather sparse, the only two articles of note being in the September 1984 'Kit Car' (Andy Bennett's build story) and the January 1986 'Kitcars and Specials' (Graham Harper's early race-tuned car), both these articles featuring Lomax 224s. So it was rather pleasant when the kitcar press started to treat Lomax more seriously, starting with a three page spread in June 1987's 'Kit Car' by Ian Hyne, currently editor of 'Kitcars International'. This piece contained some tasteful colour pictures of the demonstrators, together with a brief road test of each. The general tone of the article was encouraging. By the time 'Which Kit' magazine had started a three-part 'Project Lomax' build-up in December of the same year, sales were really beginning to take off.

In Autumn 1987, a customer from Bristol called Chris Eker started building a dark blue 224 for his girlfriend, Maura King. He really wanted a support group to help with his build, but found that there wasn't one. Dave Low mentioned that they had been trying to get someone to set up a register of owners, so Chris decided to take on the job. In Chris' own words, "I saw an opportunity for me. As an office worker (I am an accountant) I knew about databases and I reckoned it was something I could handle. So I got myself a computer, pinched a program from work, and set to. Lomax initially sent me a list of fifty or so recent addresses to whom they had sold kits and I wrote to those to get started. Thereafter, people wrote to me. Lomax used to tell people of my existence and various magazines got my name." And so The Lomax Register was born. Lomax occasionally contributed towards postage and people on the register tended to send in extra stamps and stamped, addressed envelopes, so costs were kept to a minimum.

6.3 Nigel Whall demonstrating the re-vamped 'Q-FAD' at the first Lomax Open Day. The M & G Trailers factory is obscured by the trees in the background.

Photo: Author

Increased publicity for the marque led to increased demand for the kits, and soon the demand was in danger of outstripping supply – of the metalwork at least. Brian Mumford seemed to having problems keeping up the supply of brackets and converted rear arms. Perhaps because of his remoteness from Lomax's new premises, deliveries became erratic, and Lomax were increasingly finding themselves short of vital brackets and fittings. Because of this, they turned to a small local firm called Cougar Engineering. But Cougar ran into financial difficulties. In early 1988 and faced with losing a good metalwork supplier, Nigel and Dave took the decision to buy Cougar Engineering outright and make it a part of the Lomax Motor Company. From then on, the manufacture of Lomax components began to go 'in house' once more. For a time, the metalwork side of Lomax continued to trade as 'Cougar', at least as far as their non-Lomax customers were concerned, but gradually the name 'LMC Engineering' was introduced. The original owner of 'Cougar', who had initially agreed to stay on after the take-over, left after a short while, and Dave Low assumed full control of that side of the business.

6.4 **"Did you like the test drive ?"**
Cartoon by Nik François

It was through the existence of The Lomax Register that the first Lomax Open Day took place on Saturday 14th May 1988. The weather was warm and sunny, and the Open Day an unqualified success. Owners and builders converged from all parts of the country to swap yarns, compare notes and generally poke and prod one another's cars. Chris and Maura from The Lomax Register helped marshal the arriving hordes of Lomi, and handed out name stickers to everyone so that people, whose only contact had previously been by post via The Register, could identify each other. Everyone was presented with a lunch ticket courtesy of Lomax, and lunch was taken at a small pub in Bald's Lane, opposite the end of Hayes Lane. There was even an iced celebration cake with the inscription 'Lomax Owners', courtesy of Maura ! Nigel and Dave were in attendance of course, Nigel giving rides to prospective customers in 'Q-FAD' for much of the time. The atmosphere was pure magic, and The Annual Lomax Factory Open Day became an instant tradition.

6.5 **Contemporary Lomax 424 catalogue picture**
Photo: Courtesy of Lomax Motor Co.

6.6 **The 424 was later available with a single piece bonnet**
Photo: Courtesy of The Lomax Register

6.7 These pre- and post-rebuild views of 'Q-FAD's cockpit show the great
improvement that the retrim and respray made   *Photos: Peter Cook*

6.8 'Q-FAD' on parade in her new metallic silver livery   *Photo: Peter Cook*

Motor Co. Ltd.

LOMAX REVIEW 1988

With the introduction of a greatly improved build-up manual, many very quick and high quality builds have been achieved. These high standards were much in evidence at the well attended shows throughout the year, for which special thanks should go to Chris Eker and Maura, organisers of the Lomax register, for their great efforts in bringing people together. Furthermore, Maura's culinary skills were sampled by many at the annual open day in May, when a special Lomax cake was devoured by the appreciative bunch of Lomaxers. Later in the year, they were both again in action at the Bristol Kit Car Show Club stand, where most visitors were assailed with most welcome hot drinks and sandwiches.

Newark was also a great gathering, well attended by the Lomax clan. The ' Great British Eccentrics ' were well represented by Lomaxers, (could they be anything else) Anthony Shelton and John Haden. Who said monocles were obsolete ? The prize for the best vehicle in the Lomax spirit, was awarded at this show to Peter Crawford (plus tribe) for his 243. Peter's car was chosen, for the ingenuity he had used in producing a 4 seater, 3 wheeled Lomax. He also surfaced at Sandown, complete with one wife, two kids and camping gear. We noticed at Castle Combe, that his car had grown a tow bar, could this be for the kitchen sink? Peter's prize was presented by Penn Roberts and was a years free subscription of Kit Car Magazine. He also received from Lomax Motor Company, a set of chrome manifold pipes.

Neil Spence also received recognition for his immaculate 424. Anthony Shelton was also rewarded and interestingly enough has covered 50,000 miles since building his Lomax.

At one or two events during the year, we were pleased to see Malcolm Norman's pristine 224, which definitely captures the Lomax spirit. It really has the classic look. It must be said that many striking Lomax examples arrive quite frequently at the showrooms.

In fact, we often bump into owners in the most unusual places. Recently, whilst returning from a Deja Vu photo session, in deepest Worcestershire, we were accosted by a menacing group of ramblers as we roared down the lane. " Hello " we thought, more Citroen purists complaining about adulterous treatment of 2 CV 's etc etc. But no, yet another customer had recognised the gentle rasp of the mighty Citroen Engine.

Another important event at Newark, was the unveiling of the new Deja Vu utility, which was subsequently taken to all the shows with the rest of the stable.

The prototype was an all steel vehicle (Lomax now own a fully equipped metal fabrication factory). Towards the end of the year, the glass fibre production model was on show, complete with conventional doors and full, weather gear. Orders are now being received and the first half dozen kits are in customers hands.

In September, a British Racing Green 223 was taken to Castle Combe Action Day. This car is fitted with a 650 cc engine, developing in excess of 50 B.H.P. and was seen lapping around the circuit, at a very respectable rate of knots, with absolute reliability.

At the beginning of October, a 223 / 224 and Deja Vu were driven to the Paris Kit and Custom Show at Le Bourget Airport. The 223 proceeded via Montpelier and all points South. It covered 3,500 miles at a considerable rate of knots, thanks to the tuned engine. The reaction to the range in France was quite amazing. We are used to the odd looks and smiles in the U.K., but the expressive French certainly go over the top with ' Vive La Differance ' etc. Many free drinks and meals were offered in exchange for a blast up the road.

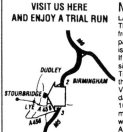

VISIT US HERE AND ENJOY A TRIAL RUN

Main showroom & technical advisory centre

LAYLAND GARAGE, Hayes Lane, Lye, West Midlands DY9 8RD. Tel: 583 2750

The map shows that our showroom is just outside Lye on the A458. If approaching from Stourbridge/M42 direction, head through Lye Town towards Birmingham passing on your left a church clock tower. Second turning past the church on left is Hayes Lane.

If approaching from Birmingham/M5 leave motorway at Junction 3 and follow the signs for Stourbridge on the A458. Along this road on the right is an adjacent Lex Tillotson/Opel Garage. First right past them is Hayes Lane. We are 100 yards on the right hand side.

Vehicles are on permanent display at our showooms and they may be viewed 5 days per week between the hours of 9a.m. and 5p.m. Monday to Friday. Saturday 10.30a.m. — 3p.m. Technical staff will be available on the first Saturday of each month, unless attending one of the major kit-car shows, where you will be most welcome to visit our stand.

At the showroom we will also be carrying limited stocks of upholstery items, brackets and accessories.

CORRESPONDENCE ONLY: BROCHURES . LITERATURE . Head Office.
Head Office: Lomax Motor Co. Ltd. 52 High Clere, Bewdley DY2 2EX. Tel: 0299 400904 Fax: 0384 374109

6.9 This **Lomax Review** appeared on the reverse of the January 1989 price list
Courtesy of Lomax Motor Co. Ltd.

CHAPTER SEVEN
That Déjà-vu Feeling

WHEN LOMAX acquired Cougar Engineering in early 1988, it was primarily to protect their source of metalwork once and for all. But having an engineering facility on tap opened up all sorts of other possibilities. Before the acquisition, Cougar had built up a number of customers' cars for Lomax, and this naturally continued. Therefore, the next step was to design an all-metal car to use the new facility's folding and spot welding equipment to the full.

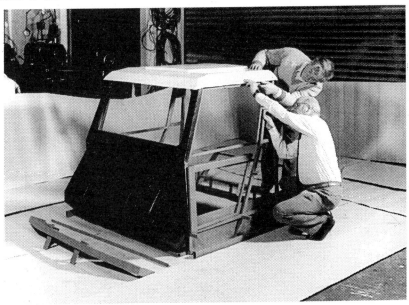

7.1 Nigel Whall and Ken Hadley assemble 'Tin Lizzie', the Déjà-Vu prototype. Note the 2CV front bulkhead incorporated into the design   *Photo: Courtesy of Nigel Whall*

Nigel decided that there would be a market for a Moke-type vehicle based on Citroën mechanics. The specification was drawn up by Nigel, but this time the styling was farmed out to a professional designer and illustrator, Ken Hadley. The original prototype of this vehicle, affectionately known as 'Tin Lizzie' and registered 'NOP 876 R', took approximately six months to build and develop, although as soon as this car was up and running, the decision was made to manufacture the outer panels in GRP instead ! It was soon to become better known as the Lomax 'Déjà-vu' when it was officially launched at the 1988 Newark show. It was to be a modular vehicle that could be constructed on 2CV/Dyane/Ami 8 running gear, have four or six wheels, a 1300cc GS engine courtesy of the Ami Super gearbox, and even three level hydraulic suspension using Citroën GS components. But although there was much interest, in reality it generated few sales. There just didn't seem to be a market for a car that did the same job as the donor, albeit looking more stylish. This was confirmed by the demise of the

7.2 **Nigel at the wheel of the completed Déjà-Vu prototype**

Photo: Courtesy of Nigel Whall

similar Van Clee, offered by a rival company at about the same time.   No six wheel or GS-powered examples of the Déjà-vu were ever built, and only thirty or so kits were sold between 1988 and Autumn 1992, when the decision to abandon production was finally made. It was a shame that the car had such an ignominious end, for all along it seemed to have great potential. The December 1989 'Kit Car' magazine even reported on a scheme by the Macclesfield-based JP Engineering Co. to bulk buy the kits from Lomax and offer fully built versions, including exports for holiday hire, but this came to nought.   Reflecting on the car's failure to attract more customers, Nigel expressed the opinion that the problem could have been that it was a large car with a small engine – but then so was the donor !   Today the Déjà-vu is a rare beast indeed, even less common than the original Lomax 224 'letterbox' cars of the early '80s.

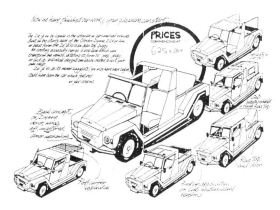

7.3 **The Déjà-Vu launch leaflet.   The drawings are by Ken Hadley, the car's designer**

Courtesy of Lomax Motor Co.

7.4   JP Engineering's Déjà-Vu prototype
Photo by David Hill, reproduced by kind permission of Kit Car magazine

7.5   Rear three quarter view of the JP Déjà-Vu prototype
Photo by David Hill, reproduced by kind permission of Kit Car magazine

The Cougar acquisition bore fruit in other ways too, for in November 1988, Lomax launched their first ladder/backbone hybrid chassis in response to the increasing number of donors with rotten chassis. Priced at £250 + VAT, this came in two versions. The standard type featured mounting points for the Citroën suspension spring cannisters and was suitable for both the 223 and 224. In addition, a second style of chassis was offered, allowing the use of coil-over shocks allied to the Citroën suspension arms. This let the car's occupants sit two inches lower than was possible with a normal Citroën chassis, and used a massive tower to mount the rear coil-over on the three-wheeler. Although the more conventional version sold well, the coil-over type did not, and was quietly dropped after a short while.

7.6 The abortive Lomax 'coil over' chassis
Photo by kind permission of 'FLAT OUT', magazine of the Citroën Specials Club

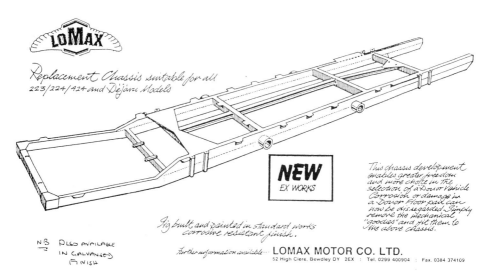

7.7 The launch leaflet for the Lomax ladder chassis

Courtesy Lomax Motor Co.

From the very earliest times, Lomax kits had been sold abroad, but from 1988 onwards, the steady trickle grew to become a flood. Agents were appointed for many European countries, including Grupo Náutico S.A. in Madrid, Spain. It was for this market that the 'Spanish', later to be called simply the 'Continental' bonnet was developed. Spanish laws relating to kit cars are more restrictive than in the UK, and one of the requirements enabling the Lomax to be sold there was that the engine had to be totally standard, complete with the original cooling system. The only way this could be achieved was with a specially designed wider-fronted bonnet which enclosed the Citroën twin, its exhaust manifold and the heat exchangers. The new bonnet option was designed with a split-line between the dummy radiator grille and the oil cooler slot, allowing it to open alligator-fashion. Naturally, the benefits of keeping the cooling fan and heating system intact, albeit at the expense of a broader front, were not entirely lost on the British buying public and the 'Continental' bonnet became a popular option from March 1989 onwards. Previously, the only way of keeping the fan and heater had been to fit the bonnet intended for the 424 - at least one car was built this way. Often seen in conjunction with this bonnet, particularly for export to countries where cycle wings are frowned upon by the authorities, are the flared front wings. These came about through an order from the Layland Brothers for a kit which they could build up into a 224 demonstrator of their own. This was to become 'TTB 252 S', the red 224 featured in the colour Lomax brochure at the time. Not liking the cycle wings, they requested Lomax make them a set of flared front wings similar to those developed for the 424. A wider set (wider because the standard bonnet is narrower than the 424 item) was produced, and these later came to be associated with the 'Continental' bonnet, although they were not originally designed to go with it.

7.8 Grupo Náutico's Continental bonnet 224 was exhibited at the Stoneleigh show prior to despatch *Photo: kind permission of 'FLAT OUT', Citroën Specials Club magazine*

The story of how Grupo Náutico S.A. acquired their demonstrator speaks volumes for Citroën's engineering. In January 1989, four representatives from the company arrived at Lye, having driven their donor car from Madrid. A bird which entered the fan casing during the journey had partially severed the wire leading to the points box. As a result, the engine had been misfiring for the last 400 miles when it arrived at Lye. The car eventually ground to a complete halt - 200 yards from the factory !

Lomax- el deportivo inglés años 30

Réplica del Morgan Four Wheeler, construido respetando los detalles y la carrocería, pero con la mecánica actual.

Especificaciones técnicas: • Marca Lomax 223 Supersports • Motor: Citroën • Origen: Bewdley, Inglaterra • Nr. cilindros: 2 opuestos • Potencia efectiva: 35 CV • Cilindrada: 602 cm³ • Peso vacío: 478 kg • Velocidad máxima: 120 km/h. • Instrumental: Reloj, indicador de carga de batería, cuenta revoluciones, tacómetro con indicador de kms. parcial y total, nivel de gasolina.

GARANTIA DE 1 AÑO: Recambios y revisión en cualquier servicio técnico de Citroën.

Grupo Náutico, S.A.

Dirección: C/. Constancia, 28, Local

28002 MADRID - ESPAÑA

Teléfonos: 413 44 53 - 413 44 97

Fax: 413 43 96

7.9 Grupo Nautica's sales leaflet. The Lomax is offered as a replica **Morgan** four-wheeler !
Courtesy of Lomax Motor Co.

Their dickey-seat Lomax 224 was built up in double-quick time, and they then drove it back to Madrid in two days. The Lomax had only been test-driven the length of Hayes Lane before they left !

Meanwhile, Lomax gained some valuable publicity from an article in the March 1989 'Kit Car' magazine featuring Ramsgate-based Anthony Shelton's seven-country, two-week tour of Europe. During the 2,500-mile journey, Anthony's 223 acquitted itself well, the only trouble being a small blow-hole in the exhaust pipe and two pints of oil consumed ! The December 1989 'Kit Car' contained the sequel - Anthony Shelton's trip to the Arctic Circle via Scandinavia.

It was at the Stoneleigh kit car show on the 1st May 1989 that an alternative club for Lomax owners was formed - The Citroën Specials Club. The original idea for a club to cater for **all** Citroën specials, irrespective of which manufacturer's kit they were built from, came from Peter Bird of Falcon Design. Together with friend and Falcon customer Gareth Coates, he attempted to start such a club but met with little success. Then another customer, Trevor Richens, agreed to have a go, initially covering the South East of England only. The first newsletter of the 'Citroën Specials Club (South East)' was despatched to twenty-nine prospective members in September 1988. At the 1989 Stoneleigh Kit Car Show the club was formed and the first officers elected. Eight years on, the club has over 550 members, many of which drive a Lomax.

The second Lomax Open Day took place on Saturday 13th May 1989, with a treasure hunt organised for the Sunday. The second Open Day was very much like the first, except that it drew an even larger crowd. On the Saturday afternoon, an impromptu run around the streets of Stourbridge was organised and led by Dave Low in 'Q-FAD', the 223 demonstrator. Again, lunch and a drink were on Lomax, this time at the 'Saltbrook End' at the bottom of Hayes Lane. Sunday dawned rather overcast as lots were drawn for the treasure hunt starting order outside the Layland Brothers garage. Lomi of all kinds were sent on a forty-mile course taking in Worcester and finishing at Wynd's Point, Malvern. The new 'Déjà Vu' demonstrator was in attendance, and was pressed into service as a camera platform from which the participants were filmed with a video camera. The route passed the Morgan factory at Malvern Link and one of the clues asked what they made there ! The 'treasure' was a gold-painted Lomax wheeltrim, cunningly concealed behind the Wynd's Point hotel bar !

7.10 The treasure hunt route passed the Morgan factory – and they asked what was **made there !**
Photo: Author

HELP!! HELP!! HELP!! HELP!! HELP!

BEN SHAWS
Mineral Water Manufacturers Since 1871

 LOMAX

are organising the antidote to the famous Beaujolais Run

"Pennines to Paris Spring Water Run"

in aid of Leukaemia Research

A Le-Mans style start featuring Lomax Sports cars is planned from Ben Shaws factory in Huddersfield at 7.30 am on May 17th and all cars are expected to arrive at the Paris destination later that day.

Your help by way of sponsorship would be gratefully appreciated. If you would like to sponsor a driver then please put your name, telephone number and amount on the list below.

DRIVERS
MAURA KING + CHRIS EKER

L E. M. Gregg   YEB 119

SPONSORS NAME	TEL. NO./ADDRESS	AMOUNT	SPONSORS NAME	TEL.NO./ADDRESS	AMOUNT
S E B Steve Bowly	Southern Electric 0628 822166 x 4486	10-00	Richard Page	Southern Electric Euston	10-00
S. Kongo	Tokai Bank	10-00	Chris Adams	Norwels	5-00
S. Todo	" "	10-00	Richard Lazarus	Schroders	15-00
Y. Harayama	" "	10-00	Ian Edwards	Midlands Electricity	5-00
Chris Taylor	Lloyds Bank	10-00	Gordon Sams / Paul Miles	" "	3-00
Mike Gorran	" "	5-00	Barclays	Barclays	100-00
Finlay Cooke	Manufacturers Hanover	25-00	John Deans	Rothschilds	10-00
Frank Shiner Tim Arrington	Midland Montagu	100-00	Gwen Batchelor	Price Waterhouse	10-00
John Kasperek	National Westminster	20-00			
Peter Pollak	Babcock & Brown	5-00			5-00
Norman Crowe	" "	10-00	Nick Kostern	SWEB	
Nicolas Littlebridge	" "	5-00	David Legg	SWEB	2-00
Mike Andrews	Eastern Electricity	10-00	Karen Bate	SWEB	5-00
Graham Dugdale	Southern Electric Eastern	10-00	Adrian Valentine-Hach	SWEB	3-00

8.1   Sponsorship form from the first 'Pennines to Paris Spring Water Run'

Courtesy of Chris Eker

CHAPTER EIGHT

Water to Paris, Coals from Newcastle

MANY LOMAX owners got their first inkling of what was to come when they received a newsletter from The Lomax Register in March 1990. A sort of 'Beaujolais Run' in reverse was being organised for Thursday 17th May. Participants were to drive from Huddersfield to Paris by Lomax, each car carrying a bottle of Pennine Spring Water, the beneficiary of all this lunacy to be Leukemia Research.

8.2 Promotional photo featuring **Nigel Smith** *(left)* **Managing Director of Suncharm,** and **Nigel Whall** *(right)*, **Managing Director of Lomax.** **The 223 on the right is** **'Q-FAD' pre-accident** *Photo: Courtesy of Lomax Motor Co. Ltd.*

The idea came from Nigel Smith, a Lomax customer and director of Ben Shaws/Suncharm Ltd., a Huddersfield-based lemonade manufacturer. The company chairman, who Nigel Smith had been very close to, had recently died from leukemia and the run was in his memory. Ben Shaws sponsored the first of what was to become many 'Pennines to Paris Runs', providing ferry crossings and hotel accomodation in Huddersfield and Paris for the occupants of fifteen cars. The run was open to anyone driving a Lomax car, including the Déjà Vu, but in the event the majority of entries were Lomax 223s. The convoy started from Huddersfield at 7.00am on 17th May and arrived in Paris the same evening. It was hoped that the famous cricketer Ian Botham would start the run, but unfortunately he was unable to make it. Nevertheless, it was a great success in that it caught the public imagination and raised a lot of money for the charity. The tired participants drove back to England the following day, and many attended the Lomax Open Weekend with their cars on 19th and 20th May.

The following is an 'eyewitness' account of the adventure, courtesy of Chris Eker of The Lomax Register: *"On 17th May 1990, about twenty cars set out from Huddersfield (including 'Bluebottle') and dashed to Paris. It was a spoof on the 'Beaujolais Nouveau' annual race. If you remember, there was a scandal at the time with Perrier Water, which was found to be contaminated with traces of benzine. Our party carried a bottle of Pennine mineral spring water which we warranted 'benzine free', and which we presented to the French in a short ceremony in Paris. It was a joint venture between Lomax and Suncharm, who bottled the Pennine water. The boss of Suncharm (Nigel Smith) had a Lomax and was a bit of a 'Hooray Henry', hence the adventure. One car blew up on the starting grid, but all the rest made it as I recall."*

8.3 All lined up for the ferry. The car in the foreground, '000 946 V' was built by its owner in less than three weeks especially for the 'Water Run', and was sold off shortly afterwards   *Photo: Courtesy of Nigel Whall*

8.4 'Kitcars International' magazine originally captioned this photo as 'Nigel Whall, rugged, action hero, speeds towards our destination' !
Photo reproduced by kind permission of 'Kitcars International' magazine

8.5 'We've made it !' Some of the participants at the Arc de Triomphe, Paris
Photo: Courtesy of Nigel Whall

8.6 Dave Low and Nigel Whall plus 'Q–FAD' at l'Hôtel
Photo reproduced by kind permission of 'Kitcars International' magazine

8.7 **A line of Lomi at the Midlands Motor Museum, Bridgnorth**

Photo: Courtesy of Nigel Whall

The Open Weekend followed the format of the previous two events, with a mass drive through Stourbridge on the Saturday and a convoy to the Midland Motor Museum, Bridgnorth, on the Sunday. A surprise guest at Bridgnorth was the young lady who had featured as a model in the contemporary Lomax colour brochure, and keen owners wasted no time in taking her picture with their own cars.

8.8 **A surprise guest was the young lady featured in the Lomax catalogue.........**

Courtesy of Lomax Motor Co.

The names of Suncharm and Lomax were linked in another way, for throughout the latter part of 1989 and up to 31st May 1990, Suncharm ran a 'Win a Lomax' competition. Entry details were printed on the sides of thousands of lemonade cans, the prizes offered being a fully-built Lomax, twenty rally jackets and one hundred limited edition Lomax 'T' shirts. Entrants had to answer three simple questions and state why they thought Suncharm soft drinks were so popular. The lucky winner received a Lomax 223, assembled not by Lomax, but by the workshops that normally maintained Suncharm's company vehicles !

8.9 **Doing the Can–Can ! These two pictures show the special Sun Charm drinks can featuring the 'Win a Lomax' competition**   *Photo: David Williams Studios, Luton*

For some considerable time, it had been in Nigel Whall's mind to create a bigger better version of his car, a kind of Super Lomax. The beginnings of this went back as far as 1987, when Lomax attended a small kit car show in a sports hall at Newport, Gwent. Business was abysmal to say the least, and only one brochure was sold over the whole weekend. However, it wasn't a complete waste of time. A locally-based American serviceman got chatting and returned after a short period with a catalogue from Nostalgia Cycle Inc. of California. This featured a kit-form air-cooled V-twin engine of some 1543cc, intended as a substitute for the Harley-Davison motor so beloved of American chopper builders. Basically a slice taken from the popular Chevrolet V-8, it used mainly Chevrolet internal parts, creating a unit for which most major spares were readily and cheaply available. Nigel studied the book with great interest. Perhaps this was the power unit he had been looking for - simple, easy to work on - and powerful !

Towards the end of 1990, Nigel's thoughts turned again towards the American engine kit he had heard about at Newport, and he set about obtaining one for evaluation. He contacted the Californian manufacturers and arranged for a fully-assembled sample motor to be freighted over from the States. It was a impressive-looking item, and Lomax

8.10 Lomax exhibited the Super Vee engine mated to a Citroën GS gearbox at several
shows   *Photo: Author*

8.11 This artist's impression by Ken Hadley, showing the Super Vee cresting Shelsey
Walsh, was drawn before the car was built.   There are many inaccuracies,
including 2CV front suspension instead of Lomax wishbones – and the engine
mounted the wrong way round !   *Illustration Courtesy of Lomax Motor Co.*

exhibited it on their stand at kit car shows throughout 1991 in order to gauge the public's reaction. The immediate aim was just to import and supply the engine, if the demand existed. The engine generated a lot of interest but no actual sales, so to show the potential, Nigel had it mated to a Citroën GS gearbox. This caused a few problems since the drive was usually taken from the nearside when it was mounted in a motorcycle frame, and in order to fit the car-type gearbox, it had to be taken from the other side. As the idea of the Super Lomax began to take shape, it was obvious that it would need a purpose-designed chassis, so Nigel designed a semi-spaceframe set-up, based around four main tubes. In the time-honoured fashion, the layout was chalked out on the workshop floor, and construction began. It was decided to give the new car a strong family resemblance to the existing model, and so the upper sections of a standard Lomax body-tub was utilised, with the cockpit shortened 11½" by the simple expedient of taking a section from the middle. Thus the cockpit area, at least, reverted to the dimensions of the first car, 'Genesis'. A lot of thought was given to ease of construction, and unlike the ordinary Lomax, both scuttle top and boat-tail were intended to be removeable panels, to aid tasks such as wiring up. With the basic ergonomics sorted out, it was time to bring in an outside consultant to design an efficient front suspension. The man chosen was Dick Buckland, already well-known for the Buckland B3 Ford-engined trike. Citroën GS front uprights were chosen, and the track was fixed at GS dimensions by virtue of the standard GS driveshafts utilised. Taking all the parameters into consideration, Dick designed an anti-dive system based closely on Formula One racing car practice, mounting the pushrod-actuated coil-over shocks inboard, above the bellhousing. No expense was spared, and detail finishing was courtesy of Bob Lewis of Projects of Distinction Ltd. He produced a superb engine-turned dashboard and outside handbrake lever, and was responsible for much of the metalwork on the exterior of the car.

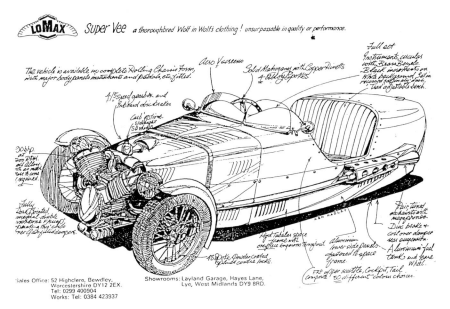

8.12 **This later line drawing is a more accurate representation of the Super Vee, although the carburettor is shown facing the wrong way and there is no alternator**
Illustration Courtesy of Lomax Motor Co.

As things progressed from engine through to engine/gearbox combination, then rolling chassis, and finally completed car, it was exhibited at various kit car shows. Together with a projected price of £7,000 to £8,000 all in, this served to create a lot of interest, from both press and public. Rather than a deliberate choice, the name of the car just seemed to evolve. When it was first shown to the public, the engine alone was marketed as the Lomax Super Vee, 'Super Vee' being the trade name under which the engine was sold in America. When it was fitted to the new three wheeler, the name simply stayed with it.

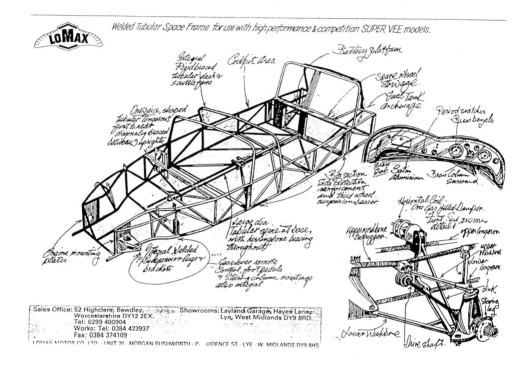

8.13 The Super Vee space frame drawn by Ken Hadley

Illustration Courtesy of Lomax Motor Co

But behind the scenes, all was not well. While the completed car looked superb, and handled and braked really well, it did not actually run reliably. Lomax had no end of trouble with the engine, a supposedly factory-assembled and ready-to-run unit. It gradually became apparent that the engine which Lomax had bought, and around which the whole car had been based, was a grossly under-developed unit with a number of basic design flaws. This was a crushing blow, especially as when it could

8.14 **This head-on view of the incomplete Super Vee shows the massive engine and Dick Buckland-designed suspension**   *Photo: Courtesy of Lomax Motor Co. Ltd.*

be persuaded to run, it was as powerful as Nigel had hoped. Throughout 1992, 'Kitcars International' magazine took a keen interest in the Super Vee, and embarassingly kept promising their readers that they would be test driving it 'soon'. But the road test did not materialise. By August 1993, with Lomax heavily involved in other projects, the decision was taken to abandon the idea of making replicas. Instead, the existing Super Vee was to be developed as time permitted, and then used as a publicity vehicle, a sort of manufacturer's concept car, to promote the Lomax Motor Company. With this decision, and the rise of the US dollar against the pound, all hopes of importing further engines and the kit form motorcycles that came with them, were abandoned.

8.15 **Nigel Whall at the Stoneleigh Show with the finished Super Vee**   *Photo: Author*

8.16 This rear view of the Super Vee clearly shows the Lomax family resemblance
Photo: Author

8.17 An underbonnet view of the Super Vee showing the pushrod front suspension
Photo: Author

8.18 A Super Vee brochure was written before production plans were shelved
Courtesy Lomax Motor Co.

NEWS INFORMATION   **Motor Co. Ltd.**   JULY 1991

Sales Office: 52, Highclere, Bewdley,
Worcestershire DY12 2EX.
Tel: 0299 400904

Showrooms: Layland Garage, Hayes Lane,
Lye, West Midlands DY9 8RD.
Tel: Lye 2750
Fax No. 0384 374 109

Lomax Motor Co Ltd., Stourbridge based manufacturers of Specialist 3 and 4 wheeled kit cars have extended their interests upward from Citreon based cyclecars.

Developments are at an advanced stage, to vastly increase performance potential particularly with the 3 wheeled versions.

The utilization of the familiar Lomax Body style [...] new tubular space frame chassis. The chassis is e[...] competition based suspension with a pedigree sta[...] developments through "Tarkus" and now Lomax.

Bolt a 90 b.h.p. 1543cc all alloy, air cooled, [...] sharp end and the result is, a blunt instrumen[...] increase the pulse rate of any 3 wheeler clubm[...] really competitive, yet safe.

The Lomax Super Vee is intended to fulfill the incr[...] a really high performance 3 wheeler in the tru[...] without detracting from the well known existing pro[...] course continue forever and a day.

Registered in England   Directors: N.V.Whall (Managing), D.P.Low   VA[...]

1

A Lomax Company spokesman says of the Super Vee: "We do not expect a high volume of sales, in the same sense that Jaguar or Mercedes would not, of their Le-Mans versions. However, the big Lomax does provide a basis for a road going high performance sports car.

"Appearing initially in comparatively detuned 90 b.h.p. form, giving 80lbs ft torque at 4500 r.p.m., with the assured backup readily available to increase output massively above these figures".

The breeding inherent in the Lomax Super Vee includes the attentions of Jake Challenger, to suspension details incorporated in "Tarkus", a three wheeled racer which enjoyed success in sprint and hill climbing events during the late 70's and early 80's. Tarkus suspension was very Brabham inspired, the car now being in the hands of Lomax and forming the backbone of Lomax performance suspension development. The final adjustments and co-ordinates concerning chassis and suspension details are in the equally capable hands of Dick Buckland, whose experience in the Three Wheeler performance arena is greatly respected.

The broad general Lomax Super Vee specification is as follows:-

> Multi tubular space frame with integral seat belt and crash
> protection zones.
> Bodywork is of combined aluminium and G.R.P.
> Disc brakes throughout, inboard at front.
> Unequal Double Wishbone front suspension with inboard coil over
> shock absorbers operating through Rose jointed linkage.
> F.W.D. through 4/5 speed gearbox.

2

8.18   The official press release for the Super Vee   *Courtesy Lomax Motor Co.*

CHAPTER NINE
The Emperor's New Clothes

IN MID-1989, Lomax appointed a Welsh agent, Les Hills of Arwel Motors in Boncath. At first, Les promoted Lomax vigorously and was on hand for the Castle Coombe Kit Car Action Day on 23rd September, giving prospective customers rides around the circuit. A special Welsh Lomax Open Day was organised for 11th November at the Penlan Holiday Village, near Cardigan, to which the local press and TV were invited. Later still, advertisements began to appear for the 'Arwel Vintage Sports Special', basically a fully-built Lomax 223 under another name. A contemporary press article mentioned that Arwel had fitted a 652cc Citroën Visa motor to their own demonstrator car and possibly this was the first Lomax so equipped. Beyond 1990, no further references to Arwel and the 'Vintage Sports Special' appeared in the kit car press. Another agent appointed in 1989 was Erik de Widt of Takoma Park, Maryland, USA, although to date American sales have been rather disappointing, possibly because very few of the small Citroën range have found their way to the States.

The crunch came in February 1990. 'Q-FAD' was being driven up Hayes Lane when it was involved in a side-on impact with another car. The damage was mainly to the front, wiping off a suspension arm, and breaking the bonnet. Although 'Q-FAD' could have possibly been rebuilt in its old form, it was decided to start with a clean sheet and build a completely new demonstrator. Only the famous number-plate remained the same. This time, Lomax's demonstrator sported an Anchusia Blue bodyshell on a Lomax ladder chassis, with matching blue-painted front wire wheels and a rorty twin exhaust system. As built, it also featured a tuned, twin carburettor, overbored (652cc) engine that had been transferred from a car bought in for resale from Peter Reason, a former customer. 'Q-FAD's' old bodyshell didn't go to waste either, this being sold to a chap in Devon, who went on to use it as a basis for an ultra-low 224 with a special chassis and suspension. The new, improved 'Q-FAD' made quite an impression on all who saw her, and resulted in a rash of orders for Anchusia Blue kits. One customer fell in love with her to the extent of commissioning Lomax to build him an exact replica. This car became known, logically enough, as 'Q-FAD's Sister'.

The new 'Q-FAD' had a very public outing in May 1990, when Nigel Whall drove from Lye to Huddersfield to Paris, and then back to Lye, on the 'Pennines to Paris' charity run. A full account of this adventure appeared in the following September's 'Kitcars International' magazine, as part of a general feature on three wheelers.

'Q-FAD' in its new form was very much a no-expense spared vehicle, and in many ways reflected the change in Lomax's clientele which had taken place during the car's first incarnation. The Lomax in all its forms was essentially a cheap and cheerful vehicle when first launched, and therefore the majority of early Lomax builds were somewhat basic. Many owners seemed to do little more than substitute the original Citroën body of their donor car for the Lomax one, leaving oil-leaks and mildly rusty chassis untouched. Due to the excellence of Citroën's forty-year-old design, this mattered little, and these cars continued to give good service. Many of these early builds carried names such as 'The Flying Bedstead', 'Mange Tout', 'Carte Blanche' and so on. In later years, this tradition seemed to wane. From about 1988 onwards, a new breed of Lomax owner started to appear, typically an older professional person with more money to spend and more time to lavish on their build. This meant a welcome hike in Lomax build standards, and some really well turned-out cars. The basic kit remained one of the cheapest on the market, leaving plenty of scope for items such as new seats and chromium-plated headlamps and exhausts. Lomax were not slow to fulfill the demand for these items, and their new demonstrator positively bristled with accessories.

9.1 (Left), 'Maid of Bits', a customer-built 224 which won many concours awards and *(Right),* the rebuilt 'Q-FAD' in all her splendour   *Photo: Lomax Motor Co.*

On the 27th July 1990, at 4.00pm, the last Citroën 2CV rolled from the production line in Portugal. Citroën had threatened to wield the axe before, but this time it was for real. Although the 2CV was no longer in production, it was obvious that it would take a long time before there was any appreciable shortage of donor vehicles. Meanwhile, there was a worldwide outcry from the owners' clubs, who asked their members to mark the occasion by tying a black ribbon to the door mirrors of their cars. This protest even extended to some Lomax owners. Interestingly, there was **one** new 2CV that was not built by Citroën, but by Lomax. Some time before production finished, a Belgian customer supplied the Lomax Motor Co. with a brand new white left-hand drive 2CV Spécial (i.e. the basic model) and a commission to build the mechanical parts from this into a new Lomax. This naturally left Lomax with a new 2CV body in stock, which was later built onto a new Citroën chassis and converted to right-hand drive. With the addition of a reconditioned engine and gearbox, this resulted in a (nearly) new 2CV, although the authorities didn't quite see it this way and issued a 'Q'-plate instead of a new registration.

9.2 **On 27th July 1990, the last 2CV rolled from the production line.......**
Photo: By kind permission of Citroën UK Ltd.

During the years of Lomax production to 1990, it wasn't just the owners and build standards that had changed, but also the donor vehicles. At first, the favourite donor was the Ami 8, principally because it possessed the advantages of disc front brakes, a more powerful engine (twin-choke carb. and 9:1 compression ratio), an anti-roll bar and heavy-duty suspension cylinders. As the Ami 8 disappeared from the scrapyards, the favourite donor became the Dyane. This was second best, in that late models featured the same engine and front disc brakes as the Ami, but not the suspension or anti-roll bar. Finally, as supplies of the Dyane dried up, the most common donor became the 2CV. However, the shortage of scrapyard Amis threw up a problem. It is advisable to fit a front anti-roll bar to any Citroën-based three wheeler, since the absence of a rear wheel on each side tends to cause excessive roll. Builders using a Dyane base could originally obtain an Ami 8 anti-roll bar and side-plates from the breakers, but by 1990 the Ami had become a very scarce commodity. Therefore, in autumn 1990, Lomax launched a reproduction Ami anti-roll bar kit, containing all the parts necessary to convert a Dyane or 2CV chassis. To be strictly accurate, the Lomax kit contained a copy of the Ami Super anti-roll bar, a much heavier item from the Ami 8's larger four-cylinder cousin. Because using the softer Dyane/2CV suspension in conjunction with the Lomax single rear wheel conversion often led to 'bottoming out' troubles, Lomax launched a rear suspension interlinking kit soon afterwards. This allowed the suspension cylinders on both sides to support the rear wheel via a rear torsion bar.

It seemed that 1990 was the year of the great Lomax giveaway, for no sooner had the winner of the Suncharm competition received their prize, than 'Kitcars International' magazine were announcing a contest of their own ! The banner headline in the November 1990 edition read 'The Great Kitcars International One Of Our Wheels Is Missing Competition', a Lomax in kit form being up for grabs this time around. Entrants had to work a little harder than for the Suncharm draw. Sixteen fairly tough questions were spread across three editions of the magazine, including such gems as 'Where had Nigel Whall spent his holiday immediately after taking part in the 1990 Pennines to Paris Run ?' The winner was announced in the May 1991 magazine. Liz François from Somerset was the recipient of £2,000 worth of Lomax kit, in dark blue.

9.3 Joyful 'Kitcars International' prize-winner Liz François receives her kit from a tearful Dave Low. Two kits given away in one year, no wonder he's crying !

Photo: Nik François

The kit could not have gone to a better home, Liz's husband Nik having recently finished building a Lomax 223 of his own. Because Nik's car was christened 'Wesley', after the character from 'The Last of The Summer Wine', it seemed only right to call the new arrival 'Compo' !

The export market really began to take off in a big way. 1990 saw the appointment of two new agents, one in Germany and a second, William Van Den Burgh, representing Lomax in Holland. William was the second Dutch agent, the first, Aris Motor Co., having lost interest by then.

9.4 The German Lomax agent's publicity. A special framework is inserted inside the bodywork to allow the Lomax to comply with stringent German TÜV regulations.

Photo: Courtesy of Lomax Motor Co. Ltd.

The December 1990 editorial of the Citroën Specials Club magazine, 'FLAT OUT', contained some interesting news: Lomax were to launch a new range of cars, powered by a choice of engines ranging from 2CV through GS flat four, to an unspecified non-Citroën unit. A prototype was promised for February 1991, but production of the existing Lomax models was to continue unaffected. Nothing more of this venture was seen in print, but all can now be revealed. Lomax had obtained an original Berkeley bodyshell and intended to take a mould from it. The Berkeley sports car was originally in production between 1956 and 1960, available with either three and four wheels. Although powered by a range of small-capacity motorcycle engines, these cars went and handled very well, thanks to their light weight and front-wheel drive. Therefore, updated with modern Citroën engines, or the flat-four Alfa-Romeo Alfasud motor, the re-born Berkeley would have been a natural for the Lomax Motor Co. But it was not to be. None of the scrapyard GS engines that Lomax obtained for evaluation proved to be in good working order, and convinced that potential customers would face the same difficulties during their builds, Nigel Whall decided to specify an entirely different power unit. He chose the Ford Fiesta engine/transmission/front suspension, but the increased engine height and the Ford McPherson struts necessitated a total redesign to the front of the car. Eventually, with other projects looming, the pseudo-Berkeley just fizzled out. As an aside, the Berkeley **was** finally re-launched as a kit car in 1993, but by another manufacturer and using the Mini engine/transmission/front sub-frame.

9.5 What might have been. An original Berkeley at Stoneleigh Kit Car Show.
Photo: Author

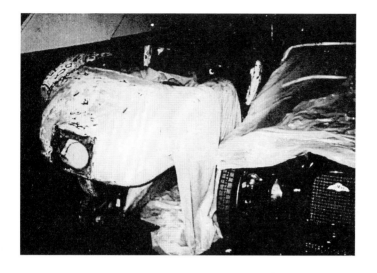

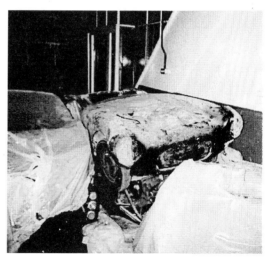

9.6 These two shots show that work on the 'pseudo–Berkeley' was well advanced when it was abandoned *Photo: Author*

CHAPTER TEN
Consolidation

THE SECOND 'Pennines to Paris Springwater Run' (6th to 9th May 1991) was very much a repeat of the previous year's event, although by the time it took place, its original instigator, Nigel Smith, was no longer working for the sponsors, Ben Shaws/Suncharm Ltd. Again, a sizeable sum was raised for Leukaemia Research.

10.1 **Brooklands – 'A ribbon of parked vehicles stretched into the distance........'**
Photo: Author

On 12th May, the Citroën Specials Club held the first of what became a series of annual pilgrimages to the Brooklands Museum at Weybridge. Sunny weather ensured a good turn out, some cars coming from as far afield as the West Country to attend. A ribbon of parked vehicles stretched into the distance along the remaining part of the old Finishing Straight, many taking it in turn to blast around what was left of the famous Members Banking. About mid-afternoon, Roger Crowhurst, club correspondent to 'Kitcars International' magazine, persuaded all those present to reverse their caps and string their cars across the banking for a group photograph. The majority of cars in the picture being Lomi, this photo was subsequently utilised for Lomax Motor Company advertisements.

10.2 The Citroën Specials Club on the Members Banking at Brooklands. This photo was later used in Lomax advertisements.
Photo: Roger Crowhurst, reproduced permission of 'Kitcars International' magazine

10.3 By 1993, the Brooklands visit was firmly established as an annual tradition
Illustration: By kind permission of John Nash

The third Lomax Factory Open Weekend was held a week later. Saturday 18th May saw the largest gathering yet of Lomi on the Layland Brothers garage forecourt in Hayes Lane. In fact, so many cars turned up on the day that it was difficult to accommodate them all in the immediate vicinity of the garage, and Lomi began to spill out onto the road outside. For the first time, Chris Eker and Maura King were not present to represent The Lomax Register, and rumours that the register was no more, were rife among those there. The rumours later proved to be partly founded on fact, as Chris Eker had expressed a wish to give up his post as Lomax Registrar, and pass the day-to-day running of the register to someone else. The register was suspended shortly afterwards, and it is a matter of regret that no-one has yet come forward to replace Chris at the time of writing. The Sunday was not blessed with the perfect weather that visitors to the previous Lomax Open Weekends had come to expect. The day dawned rather overcast with a hint of drizzle in the air, as a large party of cars gathered at Hayes Lane for the beginning of another Lomax treasure hunt. This time it was run around an entirely urban course, finishing at the Black Country Museum, Dudley.

10.4 **The grand parade paused briefly at Merry Hill – 1991 Lomax Open Weekend**
Photo: Author

10.5 **The 1991 Lomax Treasure Hunt started from Hayes Lane**
Photo: Courtesy of Nigel Whall

10.6 **The 1991 Lomax Treasure Hunt finished at the Black Country Museum, Dudley**
Photo: Author

The ACU/BMF National Rally is a motorcycle road rally with a long pedigree stretching back to pre-war days. The object of the exercise is to complete an exact amount of miles within a time limit, passing through a number of control points on the way. The course covers most of England north of the River Thames, and in order to qualify for an award, it has to be be completed within the set time of twenty hours. The rally has always had a rather under-subscribed class for three wheeled cars, originally intended, perhaps, for Morgan and BSA trikes. For the previous few years, a handful of Lomax 223s had been entered, but for 1991, the Citroën Specials Club made a concerted effort and a total of nine Lomi took part. The rally took place over the weekend of 13th and 14th July, and fortunately the weather remained dry for most of the time. The final tally was two Special Gold, four Gold, two Silver and one Bronze award, which says a lot for the cars, especially considering that one nearly ended up in a field and another completed the course with only top and second gears operative !

1991 saw yet another foreign Lomax Agent come on stream, this time Antoon Verhoeve in Belgium.

There were few changes to the Lomax range throughout the year. In 1990, the 223/224 bonnet had been changed to incorporate a larger alternator bulge as well as a slight revision to the area enclosing the front of the chassis, making it easier to release from the mould. From 1991, serial numbers were incorporated into the bodyshells. These were written onto the plywood of the boot area behind the seats, before this was sheathed over with fibreglass resin. For 224 models, the option of moulding the floor a little lower down in the bodyshell was also offered for the first time. This modification had the effect of raising the body on the chassis slightly, affording the occupants a lower seating position within the cockpit. It was around then that the words 'Stourbridge' and 'England' appeared on the Lomax bonnet badge for the first time, previous badges simply carrying the Lomax logo without any additional wording.

"*I THINK WE SHOULD HAVE STUCK TO THE MOTORWAY, NIGE'!*"

10.7   The ACU/BMF National Rally was held on the weekend of 13th and 14th July

Cartoon: John Wheatley

By the end of 1991, Lomax had rather outgrown its small premises at Hayes Lane. At this stage, the Lomax group consisted of the Lomax Motor Co. Ltd., LMC Fabrications (the part of Lomax that was formerly Cougar Engineering) and Resinject Developments Ltd., which had expanded from Nigel Whall's consultancy firm to become a general GRP manufacturer making items such as lorry mudguards and architectural mouldings, in addition to Lomax bodyshells. The premises were scattered around various sites in the district. The correspondence address for Lomax had always been Nigel Whall's home at Bewdley. The showrooms and lock-up storage were at the Layland Bros. garage in Hayes Lane. Nearby, at the Morgan Rushworth Industrial Area, Providence Street, was the unit occupied by the LMC engineering division. Finally, the RDL fibreglass factory was located some 2½ miles from the showrooms at Old Wharf Road, Stourbridge. This arrangement was less than satisfactory, involving much shuttling around the district in the course of the average working day, so the decision was taken to start looking for an alternative site where all Lomax activities could take place under one roof.

THE NATIONAL RALLY
13-14 JULY 1991

A COMPETITIVE EVENT FOR THE ROAD RIDING MOTORCYCLIST

ORGANISED JOINTLY BY THE

LIST OF ENTRIES AND FINAL INSTRUCTIONS

Jointly organised by

THE AUTO—CYCLE UNION

THE BRITISH MOTORCYCLISTS FEDERATION

and

THE CIVIL SERVICE MOTORING ASSOCIATION

OFFICIALS

Stewards of the Meeting :

Bill Smith (ACU)   Terry Reynolds (BMF)   Geoff Eteson (CSMA)

Clerk of the Course : Frank Carter   Asst. Clerks of the Course : John Hall & Colin Reeve

Chief Marshals : Anne & Keith Fryer

Results : Pam Miller & Wyn Coppock

Event Co-Ordinator : Geoff Wilson   Secretary of the Meeting : Chris Devenish

National Rally Secretary : ACU
Miller House
Corporation Street
RUGBY
Warks.
CV21 2DN (Tel: 0788 540519)

CHAPTER ELEVEN
Expansion

AT THE beginning of 1992, Lomax was restructured into three distinct limited liability companies. These were:

Resinject Developments Ltd. (RDL), wholly owned by Nigel Whall and engaged in general GRP work plus the manufacture of the fibreglass content of Lomax products.

LMC Fabrications Ltd., mainly owned by Dave Low with Nigel Whall a minority shareholder, engaged in general metal fabrication plus the manufacture of the metal content of Lomax products.

Lomax Motor Company Ltd., jointly owned by Nigel Whall and Dave Low, engaged in sales and service of Lomax products.

11.1 **The last Lomax Open Weekend to be held at the Layland Garage in 1992**
Photo: Nik François

The Lomax Factory Open Weekend celebrated its fifth anniversary on the weekend of 16th and 17th May 1992, and the traditional warm, sunny weather returned for the occasion. For the last time, as it turned out, Lomi from all over the country converged on the Layland garage forecourt. There was much to see. The Super Vee was on display, although it was not running. The yellow sectioned 'half a Lomax' 223, a familiar sight from Lomax's kit car show stands, was also outside. 'Q-FAD's old bodyshell was back again, mounted on Mike Luff's specially-made chassis and mated to a very early 224 bonnet, bought second-hand. There was even a Citroën Visa-engined motorcycle, present by virtue of the fact that it was fitted with cast aluminium 'Lomax' rocker covers, another accessory introduced by the factory circa 1989. Possibly the largest ever convoy of Lomi paraded around Stourbridge in the afternoon, jamming the nearby Merry Hill Shopping Centre in the process !

11.2 **Although not running, the Super Vee was on display**

Photo: Nik François

11.3 **There was even a Visa-powered motorbike in attendance !**

Photo: Nik François

Sunday saw a long crocodile of Lomi passing through the lanes of Worcestershire to Bewdley, where triple-parked in the High Street, they stopped for ice creams and photos. Then onwards to Nunnery Park, near Worcester, to finish up next to a giant car boot sale. After lunch, the cars dispersed to from whence they came.

11.4 **The Sunday Convoy, triple parked in Bewdley town centre. Our hero, Nigel Whall, is in the middle distance on the right of the picture – clutching two ice cream cornets !** *Photo: Nik François*

Throughout 1992, 'Kitcars International' incorporated a 'Three Wheeler' supplement in their centre pages, and naturally Lomax were featured heavily. Embarassingly, 'KCI' kept hinting that the 'Super Vee' was nearly ready for production when in reality it was anything but. However, the June issue contained an interesting snippet. Lomax had moved, but not very far ! Lomax had found a new base at Maypole Fields, an extension of Hayes Lane, at a post-war factory building called 'Endurance Works'. The new works had a floor area of some 14,000 square feet, with possible room for further expansion. As an interesting aside, Dave Low was no stranger to Endurance Works, having attended a job interview there long ago with a company producing components for the mainstream car industry.

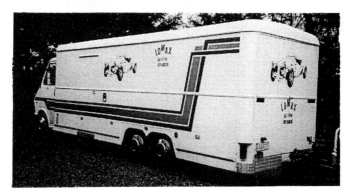

11.5 **This impressive transporter belongs to Lomax's Belgian agent, a regular sight at Lomax Open Days** *Photo: Courtesy of Nigel Whall*

WHO IS LOMAX?

In the early 1980's, Nigel Whall, an energetic creative practical engineer with a highly enthusiastic attitude towards motoring for sheer pleasure, could not resist the possibility of building a three-wheeled car. His inspiration was fired by those eye-catching examples which appeared in the late 1920's and continuing throughout the thirties. These cars gave so much pleasure to their owners through a sometimes surprising performance and also from the admiration which they invariably attracted. Nigel Whall was impelled to design and build something resembling this type of vehicle, but to make use of the more up-to-date technology which is available these days. He recognised the potentiality which the small range of Citroen vehicles were able to offer. Their popularity was centred around economy, reliability and good but eccentric design which stemmed from an internationally acclaimed quality engineering background.

Enthusiasm combined with practical skills enabled Nigel Whall to set about his project. He built the car body in glass fibre, another technology in which he had distinguished himself and become an expert in previous years.

The finished car attracted so much attention that he was forced by popular demand to produce many more, which were subject to much improvement as time progressed.

David Low, an ex-Royal Naval man came to share Nigel's enthusiasm for these vehicles. Soon they formed a team. David, with typical naval training disciplines and with a great experience of metal fabrication and assembly work, set about getting the team into 'Bristol fashion'. In the early '80s, Lomax Motor Co. Limited began to appear at Kit Car exhibitions throughout the country and a pattern of operations emerged in which David looked after the immediate needs of Lomax customers and Nigel provided the seriously technical and creative back-up.

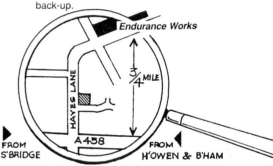

The map shows that our showroom is just outside Lye on the A458. If approaching from Stourbridge/M42 direction, head through Lye Town towards Birmingham passing on your left a church clock tower. Second turning past the church on left is Hayes Lane.
If approaching from Birmingham/M5 leave motorway at Junction 3 and follow the signs for Stourbridge on the A458. Along this road on the right is an adjacent Lex Tillotson/Opel Garage. First right past them is Hayes Lane.

11.6 How Lomax announced their move to Endurance Works in summer 1992

WHAT IS LOMAX?

In 1992 Lomax Motor Company celebrated over ten years of continual production of the products which range from 2CV based three and four wheeled lightweight cycle cars and a number of potent four cylinder Citroen engined sports cars.   Other developments have taken place in the form of inexpensive, versatile utility vehicles, also there are further projects in the pipeline which have not yet been announced. Lomax are among the founder members of the Specialist Transport Advisory and Testing Utility Society (STATUS). The company have operated in separate factories with an additional showroom at Lye, nr. Stourbridge, where demonstration vehicles are always available. Lomax have agents in many countries throughout the world.

During the summer of 1992 the first phase of a programme of expansion will take place, the object being to house the whole of the manufacturing and administrative processes under one roof. Over 14,000 sq.ft. of factory space will become the new home of Lomax. Motor Co. Limited, at **Endurance Works.**

The increased capability will allow production of the equally famous primarily Ford based Ranger and Space Ranger vehicles to be transferred from New Milton in Hampshire to

Endurance Works, which is situated at Cradley, in the West Midlands.

L.M.C. Fabrications, the metal working company which supplies Lomax with all production components for the vehicles will be under the same roof. L.M.C. also supplies many other industries with assemblies and fabrications in steel or alloys. One off, or repetition work is undertaken.

Also scheduled to make the move is, R.D.L. Resinject Developments Limited, being under the direct control of Nigel Whall have always produced the G.R.P. and F.R.P. Lomax car body shells or 'Tubs' as they are known. In addition R.D.L. is a supplier of large high quality G.R.P., F.R.P., and foam filled structures to many industries, including architectural facades, civil engineering applications and repetition work for the heavy automotive industry. Development projects for all industries are a speciality at R.D.L.

Existing Lomax owners always keep in close touch with the works. Sometimes over one hundred Lomax vehicles of all descriptions can be seen at a gathering, either for an annual Lomax event or for a sponsored charity organised from within their ranks and often supported by the works either directly or indirectly

ENDURANCE WORKS, MAYPOLE FIELDS, CRADLEY
HALESOWEN, WEST MIDLANDS B63 2QB
Telephone: 0384 410910 Fax: 0384 69574

Courtesy Lomax Motor Co. Ltd.

The first part of Lomax to be moved was the showroom, all the materials from the Layland Bros. garage soon finding a new home. This also spelled the end of the sales agreement with the brothers, Lomax's longest-serving agents. The stores then moved in, followed by LMC Fabrications Ltd. Between November and Christmas, Resinject Developments Ltd. relocated from Old Wharf Road, completing the picture. All subsequent advertising gave the Lomax Motor Company's correspondence address as Endurance Works, and Nigel Whall's home address was phased out. At the same time, production of the Lomax Déjà-vu was quietly dropped.

On Saturday 20th June, Lomax made an amazing announcement from their stand at the Newark Kit Car Show. They had acquired the trademark, rights, and tooling to make the much-respected range of Rickman jeep-style vehicles. Almost overnight, Lomax had become one of the major players in the UK kit car business. The Rickman vehicles were a total departure for Lomax, being firstly Ford rear-wheel drive based, and secondly very much at the quality end of the market, although a slightly dated design. With the package came the assistance of the company's founders, Derek and Don Rickman, until the end of 1992. The Rickman factory at New Milton, Hants., had to be emptied quickly, and over the course of fourteen days, all the jigs and tooling were transferred to Endurance Works. The moulds for the GRP parts initially went to the old Resinject Developments factory at Old Wharf Road, and the partition walls of the front office there had to be demolished in order to fit them all in ! It was generally thought at the time that Lomax had deliberately planned their move to Endurance Works to coincide with the Rickman acquisition, but nothing could be further from the truth. In fact, it was very much a spur-of-the-moment decision, prompted by the sudden availability of the Rickman product following a chequered period in their history.

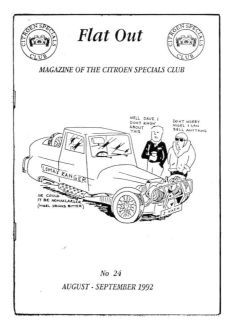

11.7 How the Citroën Specials Club Magazine, 'FLAT OUT', announced the Lomax acquisition of Rickman Vehicles *Cartoon by kind permission of John Nash*

For 1992 there was a change to the annual charity run. Ben Shaws/Suncharm Ltd. were no longer able to sponsor the run, and so the Gloucester branch of the NSPCC stepped into the breach. On 12th July, the Paris-bound participants set off from Gloucester to take part in the hastily-renamed 'Cheese Run', and for the first time, the convoy contained a non-Lomax vehicle – a solitary Marlin kit car.

Autumn 1992 saw Lomax testing the market with yet another new venture. The American firm that supplied Lomax with the Super Vee engine usually supplied it as part of a package of parts allowing their customers to build a 'psuedo-Harley-Davidson'. Lomax signed an agreement to become the UK distributors for these kit-form motorcycles, and even produced a tentative catalogue. Unfortunately, the Dollar began to rise against the Pound at about this time, and this soon made the imported parts too expensive for British pockets. For a while, it looked as if Lomax would be the only manufacturer in the country to offer kits to build two, three and four wheelers, but the unfavourable exchange rate soon put paid to that.

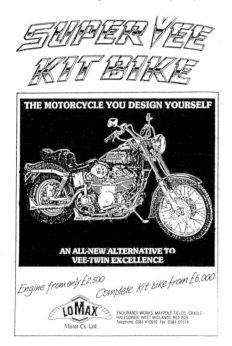
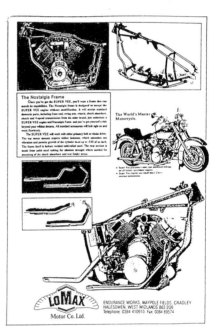

11.8 A rare catalogue for the Lomax Super Vee kit bike

Courtesy Lomax Motor Co. Ltd.

Keen to show off their new centralised factory, Lomax arranged a one-off extra Open Day for 30th December 1992. It was bitterly cold, so cold that cars were having to stop on the motorway with frozen windscreen washers, so it was all the more surprising that large quantities of Lomi arrived from all over the country with their intrepid crews. Hot coffee and mince pies were served in the showroom, whilst small groups were taken on guided tours of the production and assembly areas. Visitors were shown a pair of red Lomax 224s in the process of construction and were told that these were destined to become famous – they were to star in a TV series during 1993 !

A new television company, Carlton TV, had recently taken on the franchise for the London area and had commissioned a number of new programmes. Among them was a series called 'Frank Stubbs Promotes', produced by Noel Gay TV Productions and starring Timothy Spall. Timothy was to play the central character, Frank Stubbs, a ticket tout-turned-promoter who would take on the most unlikely projects. Among them would be a fictional kit car company called 'Lomax' ! Although Lomax featured in only one episode, preparations included buying two complete 224s (so that filming could take place at two locations simultaneously), hiring several bodyshells and a 223 (for the factory scene) and renting an empty industrial unit to equip as a duplicate Lomax factory for filming purposes. When the programme was transmitted on 17th July 1993, the factory scenes were all too brief, and the fictional Lomax company was depicted as a one-man operation run by a Scotsman. However, the publicity did the **real** Lomax Motor Company no harm at all ! Besides, Lomax had shrewdly made an arrangement to buy back the pair of 224s after filming had finished.

11.9 **Two stills from 'Frank Stubbs Promotes', starring Timothy Spall and Daniella Westbrook** *Photographs: John Brown, Courtesy of Carlton Television*

CHAPTER TWELVE
New Lamps For Old

MIRRORING the success of Lomax, the Citroën Specials Club continued to expand until, by early 1993, the membership had reached nearly four hundred, at least two-thirds of which were Lomax owners. For the first time, on the weekend of 20th and 21st March, the CSC organised a National Rally and Annual General Meeting at a Leamington Spa hotel. The weekend went very well, over eighty members attending the Sunday AGM, including Dave Low from the Lomax Motor Company. Dick Buckland, who had designed the Super Vee suspension, was the guest speaker.

Lomax's own Open Weekend at Endurance Works, on 5th and 6th June 1993, was organised for the first time as a joint affair for both Lomax and Rickman owners. As usual, the weather was fine. Over seven hundred people were expected to attend, and the food was ordered accordingly, but far fewer actually turned up. Support from Lomax owners was slightly down on previous years, and unfortunately there were only a handful of representatives from the Rickman contingent. The Sunday convoy led to the Carding Mill Valley, between Craven Arms and Church Stretton. Meanwhile, eight members of the Citroën Specials Club took their four Lomax 223s on a fourteen day circular tour of Europe, visiting six countries and five of the highest Swiss mountain passes during the 2,500-mile trip.

12.1 Citroën Specials Club 1993 European Tour. You can take a Lomax anywhere – and this picture proves it ! The author's Lomax 223 atop the Swiss Furka Pass, 7976ft above sea level. *Photo: Author*

The 1993 annual charity run was a great success. This time around, the NSPCC's head office in Birmingham organised the sponsorship, and the run was re-christened the Birmingham-Antwerp Run. 26th June saw a convoy of cars set off from Centenary Square, Birmingham, heading for Felixstowe. From Felixstowe, the ferry was taken to Zeebrugge, then onwards by road to Antwerp. There the run officially ended, but before returning to England, a smaller group of cars went on to visit the Belgian,

German and Dutch Lomax agents over the next few days. Since 1990, these Lomax-sponsored runs have raised in excess of £40,000 for charity.

In September 1993, Lomax held a sales seminar at Endurance Works for existing and prospective agents. Delegates arrived from all over the country, and were given a sneak preview of a hitherto secret project. All was revealed to the general public when the London Motor Show opened at Earls Court on 15th October. There, among the mainstream motor manufacturers, was the Lomax Motor Company stand, and on the stand was a new model !

12.2 **The Lambda styling buck undergoing development**
Photograph reproduced by kind permission of 'Kitcars International' magazine

The new Lomax Lambda represented the first significant redesign of the 223/224 range since 1983, and as such was quite a milestone in Lomax history. An outside designer, Jim Dimbleby, had been brought in to update the 223/224 under Nigel Whall's direction. With 64 changes over the old model (which, it was announced, would remain in production), the new, improved range was intended to take the whole concept upmarket. From the scuttle rearwards, the Lambda strongly resembled its immediate predecessor, although there were a number of subtle changes. Chief among these was the return to the short cockpit of the prototype car 'Genesis', and a correspondingly longer boat-tail. The rear light pods were more rounded, and mindful of the thriving export market, the moulded-in dashboard was revised to make it easier to build the kit for either right or left-hand drive. From the scuttle forward, the Lambda was very different from the old 223/224, although it was still recognizably a Lomax. Gone were the familiar Lomax 'trademark' dummy radiator grille and oil cooler slot, to be replaced by a longer, divided grille with a distinct 'BMW' appearance. The 'scallops' behind the cylinders had been lengthened considerably, and a 'power bulge' added to the top of the nose to clear the oil filler. The bonnet had been re-designed with a split line just below the bottom of the grille so that it could be raised alligator-fashion, just like the 'Continental' bonnet introduced in March 1989. Two former side panels below the bonnet sides had been joined to a chin moulding at the front to make a single-piece moulding, reminiscent of the 'undertray' fitted to the earliest 224s. To give a greater steering lock than was possible with cycle wings, the Lambda carried slim, apron-style front wings, attached to the Citroën front suspension arms and arranged to rise and fall with them, but not to turn with the wheels.

12.3 **The New Lomax Lambda 3**

Photo: Courtesy of Lomax Motor Co. Ltd.

12.4 **Lambda Left.......**

Photo: Courtesy of Lomax Motor Co. Ltd.

12.5 **....... and Lambda Right !**

Photo: Courtesy of Lomax Motor Co. Ltd.

There were changes in the chassis department too. Both Lambdas 3 and 4 could be built on either an original Citroën chassis, any replacement made to the same dimensions, or a special Lomax purpose-built chassis. The special Lomax chassis allowed conventional coil-over shock absorbers to be substituted for the standard side-mounted Citroën suspension cannisters, waist level side intrusion bars within the bodywork affording some crash protection in the cannisters' absence. The front suspension arms were modified to incorporate a revised kingpin inclination, in addition to the special mountings for the coil-overs. The name 'Lambda' was chosen for the new cars to reflect Lomax's eleven years of production, 'Lambda' being the eleventh letter of the Greek alphabet.

12.6 This frontal view shows an alternative dummy radiator grille

Photo: Courtesy of Lomax Motor Co. Ltd.

12.7 The Lambda chassis and metalwork

Photo: Courtesy of Lomax Motor Co. Ltd

NEW LAMPS FOR OLD

There were several reasons for producing the new model, but one of the most important was to have a product that could be supplied easily in knocked-down (KD) form. Lomax were looking to produce a complete self-assembly vehicle in a box - no donor parts required. At the time of writing, this policy has started to bear fruit, with several kits being supplied this way. A secondary reason behind the redesign was the prospect of gaining Low-Volume Type Approval, making turn-key factory-built cars a real possibility for the future.

The first press reference to the new Lomax was a brief item in the 'Scene and Heard' column in the November 1993 'Kitcars International'. This showed two photographs of the prototype body, one of which featured Nigel Whall sitting in the cockpit. The first road test of the fully-finished Lambda 3 demonstrator was to be found in the January 1994 'Which Kit' magazine. Interestingly, the factory Lambda 3 carried the registration 'SSV 612'. This was originally allocated to a completed 224 which Lomax had bought back from a customer, and then subsequently sold on to a new owner in Holland. The personalised registration having no use abroad, was retained by the factory and used on their Lambda 3 demonstrator.

At the time of writing, the new model looks set to become a success. A substantial quantity of orders have been received, and several builds are currently in progress. The 223/224/424 remain available as a cheaper alternative, but their eventual long term survival may be in question. Unlike many other kit car manufacturers, Lomax have weathered the economic recession well. A unique product, healthy overseas sales, and diversification into non-automotive manufacturing have put the Lomax group into a strong position.

At the August 1994 Sandown Kit Car Show, the Citroën Specials Club stand was buzzing with an interesting rumour. It was said that Nigel Whall was selling his half-share in the Lomax Motor Co. Ltd. and handing over control to Dave Low. Like many unlikely rumours about Lomax in the past, it turned out to be based on fact. On Tuesday 9th August 1994, Nigel and Dave signed an agreement allowing Dave to buy Nigel's share of the business and take full control of Lomax. David Johnson, a keen Lomax and Rickman owner, assisted Dave Low with the buy-out and became a co-director and 'sleeping partner'. The assets of LMC Fabrications (the metalworking arm of the Lomax group) were absorbed into the Lomax Motor Co., while Resinject Developments Ltd. remained under Nigel Whall's ownership. Although Nigel retained the rights to the Lomax design, Dave was given a free licence to produce as many kits as he wished. The split was an entirely amicable one.

Once again, it was time for Nigel to move on to pastures new, in this case setting up a new venture making commercial vehicle bodies called Volumax Ltd. (Perhaps the similarity in name to 'Lomax' wasn't quite a coincidence !) Until Lomax moved to a nearby factory unit in mid-1996, Lomax, Volumax and Resinject all resided together at Endurance Works and co-existed quite happily. Nigel and Dave saw each other on a daily basis, but Nigel no longer had anything to do with Lomax. Of course that wouldn't preclude Nigel from designing another car in the future. Perhaps a fibreglass monocoque with an engine of 250-300cc and 80mph performance....... But that is where we first came in - didn't we ?

12.8 The launch catalogue for the Lomax Lambda 3

Courtesy of Lomax Motor Co. Ltd.

Appendix

A Dozen Little-known Facts About Lomax : –
Cartoons by John Wheatley

o   Nearly half of the Lomax Motor Company's production is exported.

o   The one export market that Lomax have been unable to penetrate so far is France – home of the 2CV.   The French authorities make it almost impossible to register a Lomax three-wheeler there.

"THAT LOOKS JUST LIKE A LOMAX — — FROM THE FRONT!"

o   Four out of every five Lomax kits sold are three wheelers.

"NICE TRIKE, MATE – BUT YOU CAN'T BEAT THE REAL THING!"

o   Nigel Whall owns both a 1932 BSA three wheeler and Morgan F-type (Ford 10hp-engined).   He belongs to the Morgan Three Wheeler Club and has had some restoration work done to the Morgan by Bob Lewis of Projects of Distinction, suppliers of the Super Vee metalwork.

○ Some years ago, Nigel Whall bought a retired Citroën GS-engined three wheeler hillclimb racer called the 'Tarkus'. It was originally campaigned by its builder, Jake Challenger, and was once quite famous. The front suspension set-up of the Super Vee was partially inspired by the 'Tarkus'. For a long time, it resided in a corner of Endurance Works, but according to Nigel, the main reason it was bought was that it came complete with a three-wheeler carrying trailer !

○ Lomax are probably the world's largest manufacturer of three wheeler sports cars.

"PROBLY NEED TO BEEF THE CHASSIS UP A BIT, EH ?"

○ The Lomax 223 seems to lend itself to modification. One member of the Citroën Specials Club has kitted out his Lomax 223 with a supercharger. Another has fitted a 1,000cc BMW motorbike engine. A third member equipped his 223 with an 850cc four cylinder in-line water-cooled Reliant engine under a 424 bonnet. The Reliant engine's torque was tremendous, but the low gearing of the Citroën transaxle led to frequent engine blow-ups. A Leicestershire man built a Lomax 224 powered by an 850cc Moto Guzzi V-twin motorcycle engine, driving the **rear** wheels through a Toyota Celica gearbox and a Morris Marina rear axle. Unfortunately, the weight of the home-made chassis led to rather disappointing performance.

o   Lomax never officially listed the 423 as a model, but several four cylinder three wheelers have been built, including at least two which had the GS flat four shoe-horned under the normal two-cylinder bonnet.

o   In addition to their own, Lomax have also manufactured a replacement Citroën 2CV chassis for the 'Wheels' company. It is a totally different design to the Lomax ladder chassis.

o   In April 1983, 'Kit Car' magazine ran an item about Lomax in which future plans for an ultra-lightweight aluminium-chassied 223 were revealed. At the time, Nigel Whall had discovered a cheap source of suitable aluminium box-section tubing, but in the event difficulties in joining it together on a production basis made the idea unattractive.

o   Most of Resinject Developments Ltd. non-Lomax fibreglass production (e.g. architectural mouldings, lorry mudguards) is made by spraying a mixture of chopped fibres and resin into the moulds. However, Lomax components are meticulously hand laid up in the traditional manner.

"LOMANCING!"

o   Lomax enthusiasts will know the words 'Lomi', the plural of 'Lomax', and 'Lomaniac', meaning an owner who has a strong addiction to the marque. 'Lomi' was first coined by Chris Eker of the Lomax Register. 'Lomaniac' comes from a conversation that the author had with his partner, back in 1987. She accused him of having 'Lomania', and from this the word 'Lomanaic' was derived. This was subsequently popularised through the Lomax Register and spread like, well....... Lomania !

Lomax Model Designations

With the exception of the Lambda, the Lomax cyclecar model range carry numbers rather than names. The Lomax numbering system gives a description of the car, and is quite straightforward. The first figure denotes the number of cylinders, the second figure - the number of seats, the last figure - the number of road wheels. Therefore a Lomax 223 is a Citroën *two* cylinder engined, *two* seater *three* wheeler. A 444 is a Citroën flat *four*-engined, *four* seater *four* wheeler. Because of the modular nature of the Lomax range, many owners have been able to build non-standard cars by combining components from different models. For instance, although never officially catalogued, several Lomax 423s have been constructed. Four seater Lomax cyclecars are rather a misnomer, a more accurate description being 2+2, especially in the case of the three-wheeler models where the internal rear mudwing intrudes into the rear seating area.

'Genesis' - The Original 224 Prototype

Built in 1982, the very first Lomax 224 differed considerably from the production 224s which followed. A ladder frame of Nigel Whall's own design was used instead of the Citroën chassis. This was considerably shorter than the standard Citroën item, and utilised the Citroën front and rear suspension arms connected to Mini rubber suspension cones. The body was also short, the cockpit reputedly measuring 27 inches from front to rear. The nosecone was without the offside alternator bulge of the later cars, necessitating a low down nearside alternator mounting, and there was no oil-cooler slot. At the front of the car was the free-standing nosecone. Between this and the scuttle was the lift-off bonnet. Below the nosecone was the undertray, which covered the front of the chassis and extended down the sides past the driveshafts. Filling the area below the bonnet and above the sides of the undertray were a handed pair of moulded side panels. The body, moulded in black GRP, incorporated a double-skinned area in the tail, filled with polyurethane foam. The lower half of the boat-tail contained a large 'letter-box' slot into which the spare wheel was fitted, acting as a rear bumper.

A.1 These 1991 pictures show that 'Genesis' remains largely in her original form

Photos: Author

A standard Citroën fuel tank was mounted in the boot floor, above the horizontal spare wheel. Lighting was taken care of by a four-headlamp system consisting of four individual spotlamps. Most contemporary photographs show a twin exhaust system, with the pipes running along the outside of the bonnet. The car was based on a Citroën Ami 8 and had an unmodified (other than removing the air-cooling cowls) 602cc engine. Registered 'MBP 821 J', 'Genesis', as the car was later to be known, was used as a demonstrator vehicle until it was sold by Brian Mumford some time between June 1984 and December 1986. The car is currently with a private owner near Cheltenham.

The First Batch of 'Letter-box' Lomax 224s

Approximately forty of these kits were produced between late 1982 and mid-1983. They superficially resembled the prototype 'Genesis', but differed in several significant respects. The main change was that the cockpit had been lengthened by 11½ inches in order to allow the body to be fitted to a standard Citroën chassis. The polyurethane foam sandwich was omitted from the inside of the boat-tail, and the front bulkhead featured a battery shelf above the truncated passenger footwell. No brackets, other than a simple Ami handbrake fitting, were supplied with the package - the customer was left to fabricate his own. Some of these early kits were exported, one as far away as Cyprus. About half of these kits were produced in Lincolnshire by Resinject Developments, the remainder in Birmingham by the first Lomax Motor Co.

The 'Mock 223'

This prototype, which was constructed in summer 1982 by Nigel Whall, and forms the 'missing link' between the first batch of 224s and the later cars. It resembled a 'normal' Lomax three wheeler, but beneath the boat-tail, it had twin closely-spaced rear wheels, making it a four wheeled car. The rear wheel arrangement was achieved by swapping the rear suspension arms on the Citroën chassis to opposite sides. It was thought that the closely-spaced rear wheels would allow the vehicle to be registered as a motor tricycle, but when this was proved not to be the case, the idea was abandoned. The blue-green bodyshell was a modified early 224 item. The 'letterbox' slot for the spare wheel had been filled in, but because the body wasn't long enough to fully enclose the twin rear wheels, a hollow numberplate box was grafted to the rear of the boat-tail to take care of the extra few inches of tyre protruding at the back. At the front, the early 224-style undertray and side panels were retained, but the bonnet was made into a single unit by fibreglassing the nosecone to the lift-off bonnet section. An oil cooler slot was cut out below the dummy radiator grille. The car featured a twin exhaust system running along the outside of the bonnet, and continuing along the waistline. The 'Mock 223' was based on Dyane running gear and registered 'NFT 896 P'. It was subsequently dismantled and the body was discarded.

A.2 **This 1983 view of the 'Mock 223' shows the numberplate box which conceals the protruding rear wheel. Note the complete absence of rear light pods.**
Photograph reproduced by kind permission of Peter Filby and 'Kit Car' magazine

A.3 **Same body, different running gear, twelve years later in 1995. The owner has added his own rear light pods to make the car road-legal.**

Photo: Norman Higgins

The 'Mock 223' was thought to have been lost forever until, in 1995, it re-surfaced in the hands of a Stoke-on-Trent based fairground operator. It appears that, during 1983, the gentleman concerned visited Lomax in order to have some GRP mouldings made for for his fairground equipment. Seeing the discarded bodyshell, he enquired as to its fate, and was told that it was about to be thrown away. He asked if they minded him taking it, and it was duly loaded into his van. In 1985, it was re-built using the running gear from a 1981 ('X'-registered) 2CV donor.

The Lomax 223 and 224

These models were introduced in the autumn of 1983, and are still in current production at the time of writing. The 'Mock 223' showed that the body really needed to be extended in order to accommodate a rear wheel within the boat-tail, and this was achieved by adding an extra five inches - 2½" to the scuttle, and a further 2½" to the boat-tail. This gave a dual-purpose body tub suitable for building either a three or four wheeler. In addition to the extra length, the 'letterbox' spare wheel slot was deleted, and twin rear light pods added. This change indirectly resulted in a cavernous boot area, particularly on the four wheelers, since the fuel tank was moved to a new position below the boot floor, in the area formerly occupied by the spare wheel. The spare wheel was relocated to a bracket on the offside of the body. The front bulkhead was modified to make the passenger footwell the same length as the driver's, with a recess above for the battery. The front of the one-piece bonnet was restyled to incorporate a small bulge for the alternator on the offside, and a moulded-in oil cooler slot was added. The front undertray was deleted from the specification. Until at least 1987, all Lomax 223/224 body tubs, excluding the 'door' models, came from one mould. Body tubs originating from this mould can be readily identified by the mould split lines on the body sides, which mimic the forward door shut lines on the 'door' model. Pre-1987 Lomax GRP components featured full colour back-up as standard, meaning that the fibreglass was coloured all the way through, rather than just the surface gel-coat. Body tubs that were made between start of production and 1987 also had a paper rope moulded into the interior of the boat-tail (behind the seating area) to give additional strength. Later cars substituted an end-grain balsa strip for the paper rope. A significant number of early kits were ordered in 'grey primer' finish for spraying, as a cheaper alternative to self-coloured GRP, although in reality this was simply a grey gelcoat. A small defect in the bonnet mould gave rise to the 'hair on the bonnet' which appears near the nosecone on the nearside. This flaw continued to appear until after 1987, although owners have often removed it along with the joint lines on the body.

A.4 This close up of 'Q–FAD's nose-cone shows the pre–1990 bonnet with the smaller alternator bulge   *Photo: Peter Cook*

A.5 Post '85 Headlamp Bracket with the outrigger tube to the top surface of the chassis   *Photo: Peter Cook*

The metalwork supplied with kits manufactured before 1985 differs from later production. The headlamp frame was in the form of a 'U' made from thicker tubing than the present item, and intended to be bolted to the front rail of the Citroën chassis, using the front bumper mounting holes. Later headlamp frames acquired a pair of outrigger tubes to connect with the top surface of the chassis. These frames were designed to be attached much further back on the chassis, approximately level with the cylinders. Pre-'85 front mudguard brackets were basically a 'P' shape, and were mounted on the inertia damper mounting lugs on the front steering swivels. Later mudguard brackets had the tubing bent to more of a 'loop' shape, and came in two versions – one for mounting as above, and one to be mounted onto the steering arm bolts, for later donors on which the inertia damper mounting lugs were absent. The scuttle frame was introduced by Brian Mumford, although some earlier cars have been fitted with one retrospectively. From 1985, a Lomax 'exhaust system' was offered. This consisted of a modified Citroën inlet/exhaust manifold from which the hot-spot tube had been removed (to allow for alternator fitting), and to which the Citroën heat-exchanger tubes had been brazed. The modifications to this unit allowed a standard Citroën exhaust system to be fitted to the Lomax for the first time. The first attempt at wet weather gear was a fixed windscreen made from an 'E'-section aluminium extrusion and introduced late 1983/early 1984. This was reputedly a unit from a beach-buggy called the Kingfisher Kustom, that just happened to be the correct width for the Lomax body. In 1988, the familiar fold-down screen was introduced to replace it. Very few earlier cars were built up with full weather gear because a windscreen, hood frame, hood and all the other associated bits and pieces cost almost as much again as the basic bodyshell kit.

A.6 **The post-'85 'loop shape' front mudguard bracket for mounting to inertia damper mounting lugs on front swivels** *Photo: Peter Cook*

From late 1986, the 223/224 gained a new option - doors. The mould was produced by modifying a standard body tub, and some of the fine detail in the front bulkhead area was lost in the process. The doors had a swept back appearance, reminiscent of those fitted to the Triumph TR3 of the '50s. The Lomax doors were generally mounted to the body using external hinges of the Mini-van type.

A.7 **The difference between the Continental bonnet** *(left)* **and the standard bonnet** *(right)* **is clearly shown in this photograph of two otherwise identical cars.**

Photo: Author

For 1987, optional flared apron-style front wings were introduced, together with wire wheels, although with the wheels costing over £300 per pair, they had few takers at first. 1988 saw the introduction of the Lomax ladder frame, a necessary measure to counteract the increasing number of late Citroën 2CV donors with terminally rusty chassis. An alternative, wider 'Continental' bonnet, enclosing the fully-cowled Citroën twin, was available from March 1989. This had a shut line between the dummy radiator grille and the oil-cooler slot, enabling the bonnet to be opened alligator-fashion. At about this time, cast rocker box covers bearing the Lomax logo, were offered as a replacement for the Citroën items. Reflecting the dearth of Ami donors available in the scrapyards, Lomax introduced a reproduction Ami anti-roll bar kit in the autumn of 1990. This was followed shortly afterwards by a rear suspension interlinking kit for the three wheelers. The 'hair in the gelcoat' disappeared from the bonnet for good when the bonnet moulding was revised slightly in 1990. In response to customers' requests, the offside alternator bulge was increased in size to allow the fitment of larger, non-Citroën, alternators. At the same time, the area at the bottom of the nose-cone (covering the front of the chassis), was altered slightly to make the completed bonnets easier to release from the mould. Lomax 'winged' bonnet badges, initially available in 1987, began to carry the word 'Stourbridge' below the Lomax logo from about 1991. At this time, serial numbers were first marked into the fibreglass of the bodyshells, (on the boot floor just behind the seats) and bulkhead serial number-plates began to appear. By 1992, a whole host of parts and accessories were being offered, including instruments, headlamps, brake, oil and fuel lines, custom-made seats, a 652cc conversion, two alternative exhaust systems, and so on. In excess of 2,000 of these kits have been produced, the majority of them 223s. At the time of writing, the kits remain in current production.

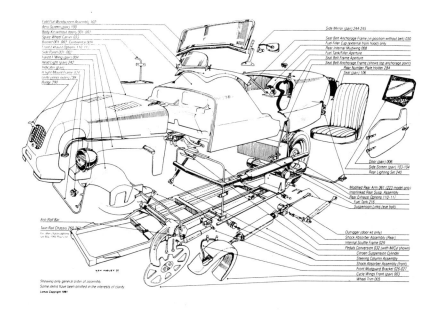

A.8 **Anatomy of a Lomax: this 1991 exploded diagram shows the options available**
Courtesy of Lomax Motor Co. Ltd.

A.9 **Lomax 223, plan view !**
Photograph reproduced by kind permission of 'Kitcars International' magazine

The 'Counterfeit' Lomax 223 and 224

During the spring of 1984, a number of unauthorised Lomax bodies were produced by Peter Bird, Nigel Whall's erstwhile business partner, in order to fulfil outstanding orders that were left when their partnership was dissolved. The copies were made by taking a mould from a genuine Lomax shell and then making some modifications. Chief amongst these were the deletion of the instrument pod on the dash, and the substitution of a flat panel. The split lines on the mould were reputedly arranged differently to those on the genuine article. No details exist of what metalwork was supplied with these kits, but presumably it was the same as that supplied for genuine Lomax kits at about that time. The amount of counterfeits produced is open to conjecture. The author knows of two certainties, and a third which may or may not be genuine. A figure as high as eighteen has been mentioned.

A.10 **Believe it or not, this car started life as one of the 'counterfeit' Lomax kits. The Pre-'85 front mudguard and headlamp brackets can be clearly seen. The passenger seems to have been on a diet though !** *Photo: Nik François*

The Lomax 424

After a long gestation period, the Lomax 424 became available in 1985. Designed for the running gear of the Ami Super, this car was a potential flyer - especially if the 1299cc unit from the Citroën GS was substituted for the standard Ami Super 1015cc flat four. The body tub of the 424 is identical to that of the 223 and 224, it is only from the scuttle forward that the four cylinder car differs. From the outset, it was realised that the flat four could not be expected to run reliably without its fan and air ducting, and so a bonnet which would enclose the full width of the engine had to be designed. The first attempt at this produced a three-piece assembly with a bulky front nosecone and a 'butterfly' centre-hinged bonnet. From late 1987, an alternative single-piece moulding was developed. The front of the bonnet was produced 'blind', leaving the builder to decide the shape and size of the dummy radiator grille and cut it out himself. The two bonnet styles were offered concurrently for a while until the first type was discontinued. The extra bulk of the front end precluded the use of the standard 223/224 headlamp frame, and so a handed pair of headlamp brackets was produced instead. To echo the styling of the wider front, a set of flared, apron-style front wings, unique to the 424, were introduced. Compared to sales of the 223/224 kits, 424 sales were few, the extra complexity of the four cylinder car tending to discourage potential buyers. In recent years, Ami Super donors have become hard to find, making the build-up a more difficult process involving adapting a GS engine/gearbox unit to 2CV or Dyane running gear. Nevertheless, the kit remains available for those who want it.

The Lomax Déjà-vu

Launched at the Newark kit car show in June 1988, the Déjà-vu was a complete departure from previous Lomax models - a utility-type vehicle based on the 2CV, Dyane or Ami 8 running gear. The construction method consisted of adding a Lomax-supplied tubular steel framework to the basic Citroën platform and attaching a series of GRP panels. The modular design was intended to offer the constructor the possibility of making anything from a bare-bones open Moke-style vehicle to a fully-enclosed car with a hard top and doors. A total of six variants were officially available. The Budget Buggy was the most basic, followed by the Déjà-vu which incorporated a roll-cage. The Sombrero included doors and a cab hard top, leaving the area behind as an open pick-up bed. The Twin Top Sombrero offered a full-length hard top and sides, rear door, rear roof support *and* an additional soft top for summer motoring. All the above models could be based on the four-cylinder Ami Super if desired.

Catalogued, but never produced, were a further two variants - the Power Lux and Power Lux 6. The Power Lux was to feature a Lomax-designed spaceframe chassis, intended to take the full running gear of the Citroën GS, including the three-level hydraulic suspension. The Power Lux 6 was to be a six-wheeled version incorporating an extra pair of trailing wheels. Approximately thirty Déjà-vu kits were sold between their 1988 introduction and autumn 1992 when production was halted.

The Lomax Super Vee

From as early as 1987, it had been Nigel Whall's intention to develop a 'Super Lomax' three wheeler to augment the smaller cars in the range. Since the mid-'80s, an American firm had been producing a 1543cc air-cooled V-twin motorcycle engine, utilising Chevrolet internals, as a cheaper substitute for the Harley-Davidson

A.11   **The massive Super Vee power unit**
Photograph reproduced by kind permission of 'Kitcars International' magazine

motor. Nigel imported one for evaluation in late 1990, and during the course of 1991, it was mated to a Citroën GS gearbox.   Next, a spaceframe-type chassis with racing car-style pushrod front suspension was constructed around this engine/gearbox.   During 1992, a body was added to the chassis and the car began to take shape.   The top half of the body was taken from the 223/224, although the cockpit was considerably shorter - a throwback to the first 224 prototype.   Below the waistline, the spacefame was panelled in aluminium.   Forward of the scuttle, a Morgan-type bonnet left the big V-twin exposed.   The machine had a powerful, purposeful look but still retained a definite Lomax family resemblance.   The projected price in 1992 was £7,000 to £8,000 including a brand new V-twin engine.   Although some sales catalogues were printed and production plans were well advanced, serious engine reliability problems called a halt to the project. By August 1993 the decision was made to finish the prototype when time allowed, but not to make any replicas.   What might have been a giant among sporting three-wheelers ended up as a pygmy.   The Super Vee remains at the factory awaiting further attention.

A.12   **The massively-constructed Super Vee Chassis !**
Photograph reproduced by kind permission of 'Kitcars International' magazine

The Lomax Lambda 3 and Lambda 4

By autumn 1993, the Lomax 223/224 had enjoyed an unbroken ten year production run, more or less unchanged. It was therefore decided to modernize and update the cars without altering their essential character. Successful modifications made by owners to their 223s and 224s over the years were taken into account when the new cars were in the design stage, resulting in a much more developed vehicle. The new Lambda 3 and 4 range was officially launched at the Earl's Court Motor Show on 15th October 1993.

The bodyshell was an update of the 223/224 item, the proportions being improved by shortening the cockpit and lengthening the boat-tail. At the same time, the rear light pods were given a more rounded and streamlined appearance. Another innovation was a pair of moulded-in recesses in the top of the boat-tail for the upper seat belt mountings. Mindful of the extra side impact protection demanded by the new chassis, bereft of the Citroën suspension cannisters, side anti-intrusion bars were incorporated into the bodywork. A change of dashboard made the Lambda the first genuine Lomax kit that was instantly adaptable to right or left-hand drive. Paradoxically, the 'counterfeit' 223s and 224s produced by Peter Bird ten years earlier had a similar feature. The front of the car underwent a radical revision. Gone was the single-piece bonnet of the previous model, to be replaced by a two-piece unit incorporating a split-line above the front number-plate. This allowed the bonnet to be opened alligator-fashion, a lesson learned when the 'Continental' bonnet was added to the range of 223/224 options. A new nosecone incorporated a long, narrow divided grille, reminiscent of the pre-war BMW 328 and replacing the separate 'radiator' and oil-cooler slot. The section of bonnet behind the front numberplate was joined to the former side-panels to make a single GRP moulding. This reduced the number of fibreglass panels ahead of the scuttle from five on the earliest 224s to three on the later cars and just two on the Lambda. A new design of apron-style front wings was incorporated, these wings being attached to the front suspension arms so that they moved up and down with the suspension but did not turn with the wheels.

The body was designed to fit either a standard Citroën chassis or a special purpose-made Lomax ladder frame. The Lomax chassis allowed the use of coil-over shocks in place of the Citroën side-mounted canisters, and a much lower seating position within the body. A novel feature was the factory modification of the front suspension arms to restore the original Citroën kingpin inclination with the lowered suspension. This resulted in lighter steering and an improved turning circle. A choice of five different purchase options, ranging from a basic bodyshell to a comprehensive kit including a remanufactured engine and gearbox, were offered by the factory.

The Club Scene

The Lomax Register

The original organisation for Lomax owners was the Lomax Register, formed by Chris Eker in Autumn 1987, following a false start in April 1986 by Ian Reid. This wasn't so much a club as a list of names and addresses of Lomax owners, together with brief comments on their cars. The object of the register was initially to enable owners to make contact with each other, and later, to allow owners to trace the previous history of their cars. Remembering that when the register was started there were perhaps only fifty Lomax cars on the road, the Lomax Register fulfilled a very useful function. Support from fellow builders enabled many cars to reach a roadworthy state sooner than might otherwise have been the case. No membership or registration fee was levied, postage and stationery costs being met by a combination of donations from members and some support from the Lomax factory. The Lomax Register was suspended in summer 1991, with over two hundred cars on the books, due to the founder losing interest in the project. It is hoped that the Lomax Register may be revived again at some time in the future.

The Citroën Specials Club

The original idea of forming a Citroën Specials Club came from Peter Bird, formerly Nigel Whall's business partner in Lomax, and later the proprietor of Falcon Design, producing a range of Citroën-based Lotus Seven-styled kits and do-it-yourself plans. Since it was initially supported by Falcon and given a section in 'Falcon News', a factory-sponsored newsletter for Falcon customers, it would have been very easy to make it a club exclusively for Falcon owners. However, Peter Bird was determined to start an any make and any Citroën Specials Club, and therefore threw it open to other makes – including Lomax. Together with friend and Falcon customer Gareth Coates, Peter attempted to promote the idea of a club throughout the latter part of 1987 and most of 1988. Unfortunately he had little success, until he mentioned the prospective club to Trevor Richens, a Falcon plans customer from Staines, Middlesex. Trevor agreed to try starting a branch of the club in the South East, initially within a twenty-mile radius of his home.

In September 1988, Trevor sent a tentative 'Citroën Specials Club (South East) Newsletter' to twenty-nine addresses, some of which were provided by the Lomax Register. The response was very good, mainly due to Trevor's infectious enthusiasm, and on 1st May 1989 the national Citroën Specials Club (by now the 'South East' suffix had been dropped) was officially formed at the Stoneleigh Kit Car Show. The new club and the Lomax Register co-operated a lot in the early days, always booking adjacent club stands at kit car shows to ensure a large parking area for like-minded enthusiasts. There was never any real rivalry between the two organisations, especially as a significant proportion of Lomax owners on the Register also belonged to the Specials Club. Spoilt for choice as to which stand to park on at shows, it was often a case of whichever stand had more room. As the Citroën Specials Club prospered, interest in The Lomax Register started to wane, in many cases because the register was just that – a register rather than an active car club. As noted above, the Register was finally suspended in summer 1991. Today, the 550-strong Citroën Specials Club remains an independent society for owners of any Citroën special or kit car, and even non-Citroën cyclecars are welcomed. However, it must be admitted that the Lomax is the most popular choice amongst members.

A.13 A typical line-up of Citroën Specials Club members and their cars. From front to back are: Lomax 223, Home-built special, Falcon LX3, Lomax 223, Mini Special, Lomax 223 *Photo: Author*

Inside Lomax
30th October 1992

IL.1 A general view of Endurance Works, taken from Maypole Fields

Photo: Author

IL.2 The showroom at Endurance Works, Triumph TR6 and Morgan *(left)* are Nigel Whall's personal cars, a Rickman Rancher is in the background   *Photo: Author*

IL.3 Through into the factory, and the first thing you see is row upon row of engines, gearboxes and suspension   *Photo: Author*

IL.4   The production area for built-up kits.   Just out of view on the left are the stores.
The dismantled car *(left)* with the wire wheels is the Super Vee   *Photo: Author*

IL.5   From the production area, we progress to the metalworking shop.   The jig in the
foreground is for the Rickman chassis   *Photo: Author*

IL.6   Propped up in a corner of the factory – the remains of the Tarkus hillclimber
Photo: Author

APPENDIX

THE FOLLOWING PICTURES WERE TAKEN AT THE R.D.L. FIBREGLASS SHOP JUST BEFORE IT WAS RELOCATED FROM OLD WHARF ROAD

RDL.1 A general view of the production floor. The chopped fibre and resin spraying equipment used, for making non-Lomax products, is at the back of the picture.   *Photo: Author*

RDL.2 A pair of body tubs, recently sprung from their moulds. In the foreground is a standard tub, in the background – a tub with door apertures, and between them is the mould for the 'Continental bonnet'.   *Photo: Author*

RDL.3 Another view of the freshly-moulded tub *(right)* and its mould *(left)*. On top of the body mould is the 'Continental bonnet' mould. In the left foreground is the internal rear mudwing mould. A casually-dressed Nigel Whall can be seen in the background.   *Photo: Author*

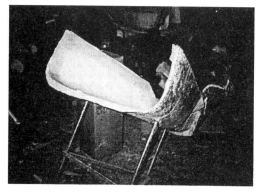

RDL.4 The Lomax 223/224 bonnet mould   *Photo: Author*

RDL.5 A freshly-moulded body tub with door apertures   *Photo: Author*

RDL.6 A body tub in the process of being laid up by hand   *Photo: Author*

RDL.7   Front wings and side panels in the process of being laid up   *Photo: Author*

RDL.8   This picture tells a tale.   That large lump on the top shelf is the **424** bonnet
mould.   It cannot have been used very often if it is stored up there !

Photo: Author

MOTOR COMPANY

Circa 1985 onwards

Motor Co. Ltd.

Early 1987

Motor Co. Ltd.

1988 Onwards.......

Above: How the Lomax Trade Mark has evolved over the years